Getting It Right

The Real Problem and God's Perfect Solution

Dr. Mike Fabarez

ISBN 978-0-9816293-4-6

For information on this publication please contact:

Focal Point Radio Ministries
P.O. Box 2850
Laguna Hills, CA 92654
(888) 320-5885
FocalPointMinistries.org

Contents

Introduction

We have a problem. We may prefer to ignore it. But we all have one, a big one. We may not all initially agree on a definition of what the problem actually is, but most will agree something is wrong – in many ways, profoundly wrong. Most of us stay busy enough to not be preoccupied with it, but when we know something's wrong, we'd be unwise to live as though it wasn't.

It is fair to say that the Bible is all about this problem and how God sets out to fix it. You may be used to hearing the "Bible-quoters" talking about the problem of "sin." That is what the Bible calls it, but before you dismiss this term as part of their guilt-inducing religious rhetoric, it would be important to understand what the Bible means by "sin." Scholars who have set out to write on the topic have attempted to summarize the Bible's diagnosis of our problem as life in a world that "is not the way it's supposed to be."[1] Or as my dad used to say, "It's a lot of imperfect things in an imperfect world."

It is hard to argue with that. While we can all point to "good days" in our lives, we have to admit that life on this planet is certainly not the way we sense it ought to be. It is filled with less-than-perfect people and experiences. A look through today's

---

[1] For instance see Dr. Cornelius Plantinga, Jr.'s, *Not the Way It's Supposed to Be: A Breviary of Sin* (Eerdmans Publishing Co., 1995).

newspaper will persuasively attest to that. And an honest assessment of our own lives will argue the point as well. While some may look into the cameras and say they've lived life with "no regrets", we have to wonder how that squares with all the broken relationships, dilemmas, sicknesses and problems which are inherent in every life. Some do work to ignore the problem. Others have come to tolerate a certain level of perpetual imperfection. But there are times when the problem cannot be ignored. "Wrong" seems to explode in our lives and we are left longing for something different.

Deep down we want to be better than we are, and we desire a world that is much better than it is. The Bible tells us that our current existence can't possibly satisfy this natural craving. As one Oxford Professor put it, *"If I find in myself a desire which no experience in this world can satisfy, the most probable explanation is that I was made for another world."*[2] This alternate reality is the gist of the story and message of the Bible. There is more than this life. There is something different. There is something much better.

But let me say right up front, the biblical remedy for the problem of sin is not achieved by working harder to fix ourselves and those around us. The predicament is too profound to be fixed by mere human effort. God's solution is much more thorough

---

[2] C.S. Lewis, *Mere Christianity* (Macmillan Publishing, 1968), p. 106.

and permanent than our willpower. God's solution is not "trying harder to be good" while persuading others to "shape up."

More rules and more effort are not the remedy. The real fix is the gospel – something God has accomplished, which has the ability to fix things on a whole other level. Think about it,

> *We do not wish either to be, or to live among, people who are... honest or kind as a matter of duty: we want to be, and associate with, people who like being... honest and kind. The mere suspicion that what seemed an act of spontaneous friendliness or generosity was really done as a duty, subtly poisons it... The whole purpose of the 'Gospel' is to deliver us from morality.[3]*

God wants to radically transform who we are and how we live. He wants to get us fired up and prepared for a new kind of reality that he has promised to inaugurate worldwide. This fix for the problem was hinted at soon after the problem surfaced in Genesis chapter 3. God said that though there would be an

---

[3] C.S. Lewis, *English Literature in the Sixteenth Century* (Cambridge, 1944), p. 187 as quoted in John Piper's address, *Lessons from an Inconsolable Soul* (Desiring God Conference, 2010).

extended period of struggle, sin, pain and death, that a profound solution would be made available soon. His plan, which would unfold in the ensuing chapters, would obliterate the problem and by the last two chapters of the Bible would bring us back to "the way things ought to be."

That's the big picture. And you can be a part of it. You can be made right and you can have a place in a world made right. But you have to accurately understand the essential components of God's solution. You have to examine carefully what God says about how we have participated in the problem and what needs to be done to embrace the fix. That's what the following pages are all about. So let's leave behind our preconceptions of religion in general, and Christianity in particular, and let's go back to what the Bible says about you and I getting it right.

Chapter 1
It All Starts with God

Elsewhere I have explained my logic of deferring to the Bible as our exclusive, sufficient, unchanging and infallible source of authority for understanding God, ourselves, salvation and a variety of other aspects of our existence.[1] If the Bible is God's inscripturated truth intended to inform and guide us, then we should start where it does – at the beginning. Genesis 1:1 tells us, "In the beginning God created the heavens and the earth."

God Created Us

Such an admission, if we are bold enough to embrace it, comes with a myriad of implications. It certainly establishes the pecking order in the universe. If God is really responsible for our existence – if he designed our neuron transmitters, our endocrine system, our skeletal structure and animated us with a thinking, rational mind – then he is "the Boss of us." He is, by virtue of his position as Creator, in charge of us. He retains the rights, he makes the rules, and he can call us to account for breaking his rules.

Consider the "sovereignty" we had over the model airplane that we saved for, purchased, and spent hours constructing at the desk in our bedrooms,

---

[1] Mike Fabarez, *Why the Bible?* (Focal Point, 2010).

how much more authority does God have to do as he pleases with his creation. And just as my mom used to wince when I decided to destroy my model plane in the backyard, we may be uncomfortable with a "Sovereign" who chooses to impose this consequence or that reality upon us; but who can cry foul if we are really his creation, living on his planet within his universe and are the result of his creative work.

I am not suggesting that this is a comfortable truth, but if it is true, we have to come to grips with the fact that God is undeniably in a position to make the rules and to enforce his chosen consequences. Admittedly, if nothing created everything, then nothing is "the Boss of us," and we are accountable to no one. This might lead to a temporary sigh of relief, considering that we'd face no fear of judgment, no accountability and no lasting consequences for how we choose to live our lives. But it would also leave us without a solution to our nagging problem – life on the planet is clearly not what we perceive it ought to be. And it would also introduce a few other problems because if we hold to this view our existence is meaningless, we have no purpose, real justice does not exist and our perceptions of love, morality, divinity and conscience are completely irrational and inexplicable.

Of course many have sought to explain our existence without reference to God. And no one can argue that it's not trendy to claim to be an atheist in a number of subcultures within our society. However, the Dawkins and Hitchens of the world are pushing a rock up a hill when it comes to persuading the vast majority of people, because most have great difficulty in reconciling a Godless reality with the built-in perception of a transcendent Creator held by billions of individuals all over the world.

As the Bible puts it, to overcome this built-in perception, people need to "suppress the truth" and "deny" their most fundamental sensitivities to God's witness in their world and in their conscience.[2] Of course Romans 1 tells us that many are successful in denying what they innately perceive to be true about the existence of a personal Creator, but this is not done without much effort. Affirming the reasonableness of God's existence is for another time (and usually for a smaller audience)[3] but it is sufficient here to point out that there are some humbling implications when we admit that God does exist.

We Were Created to Relate to God

There are also some dignifying implications if God designed and created us. One of the most significant descriptions in the creation account of Genesis 1 is the way in which God decided to set human beings apart from the rest of his material creation, by giving them the capability of relating to him personally. The Bible describes the creation of humans as being

---

[2] See Romans 1:18-32 and Romans 2:14-16.
[3] See works such as William Lane Craig, *Reasonable Faith* (Crossway Books, 2008); Alister McGrath, *Intellectuals Don't Need God & Other Modern Myths* (InterVarsity Press,1993); Francis Schaeffer, *The God Who is There* (IVP Books,1968).

"in God's image."[4] This, of course, does not refer to his physical form because the God who created us in Genesis 1 is not a physical being.[5] This "image" speaks to our capacities which set us apart from the rest of the creation – our self-reflexive and creative intellects, our emotional capacities that feel in a manner akin to God, and our volition or will that is self-directed and not simply instinctual.

This unique human composition gives men and women a capacity to relate to God unlike any other part of the physical creation. Our God-like "spirit" (i.e., the software which animates our biological hardware) was created with the privilege of being able to know and have an intimate relationship with our Creator. Though this privilege was forfeited by the third chapter of Genesis and the human race has never been the same, God promised that he would work to restore this kind of personal fellowship. However, the full restoration of our relationship with God will have to wait until this world is swapped out for the next one.[6]

This is an important observation, because it would be wrong to leave the impression that "getting it right" in this life is the full consummation of what the Bible is intending to accomplish. We can have our relationship restored with God now, but it is only a partial restoration. Consider how the Apostle John

---

[4] Genesis 1:26-27.
[5] See John 4:24 and Luke 24:39.
[6] 2 Peter 3:13.

explains this truth to those who have been reconciled to God in this life, *"Beloved, we are God's children now, and what we will be has not yet appeared; but we know that when he appears we shall be like him, because we shall see him as he is"* (1Jn.3:2). Or as Paul writes, *"For now we see in a mirror dimly, but then face to face. Now I know in part; then I shall know fully"* (1Cor.13:12). Clearly our face-to-face encounter with Jesus Christ will usher in a new reality and will consummate the relational intimacy that is intended by God's redemptive work.

God is Holy

The first five books of the Bible, which God used Moses to inscribe, go to great lengths to demonstrate that the God who created us is morally perfect, without any defect or error in his actions, attitudes or behavior. The word that reappears over and over again is "holy", which means "set apart." In his character, God is set apart from all that is imperfect or deficient. As it's put in Deuteronomy 32:4, *"his work is perfect, for all his ways are justice. A God of faithfulness and without iniquity, just and upright is he."*

Some might object to the phrase "his work is perfect" considering how poorly things have worked out down here on earth; we look around and see plenty that is imperfect. But it wasn't like this when God first created it. At the end of Genesis 1 God's own summary of what he had created was that everything he made was "good" – including the people. So whatever it was that went wrong in Genesis 3 with Adam and Eve's disobedience, the fault was not due to a defect intrinsic to the way God created them. The people God created were good and morally perfect, but they used their capacities to become unholy, imperfect and disobedient.

Their disobedience messed up the created order, but it did not impinge on God's perfection. The Bible consistently clarifies this point with rhetorical questions like: *"What if some were unfaithful? Does their faithlessness nullify the faithfulness of God? By no means! Let God be true though everyone were a liar, as it is written, 'That you may be justified in your words and prevail when you are judged'"* (Rom.3:3-4). God remains morally perfect though he works throughout redemptive history with and for the good of fallen and rebellious people.

God is said to maintain his moral perfection and holiness even though he has affixed appropriate and painful consequences for the sinful world. In this sense his holiness is even more pronounced. God is completely unlike his fallen creatures who have chosen to be morally rebellious. Whereas God always does right, all people, to one extent or another, choose to do wrong, compromise, and seek freedom from their mandated compliance to moral good.

Even so, God repeatedly instructs that his creatures be morally good. For instance Leviticus

19:1-2 tells us, *"And the Lord spoke to Moses, saying, 'Speak to all the congregation of the people of Israel and say to them, You shall be holy, for I the Lord your God am holy'."* This is a familiar refrain throughout the pages of the Bible, but unfortunately it reminds us that we are not measuring up. We may seemingly have our good moments, but when we really ponder the moral perfection of God, we recognize we aren't good enough. And that, by the way, is essential. We can hardly embrace the solution which God extends, until we fess up to the problem. More on this later.

God is Just

Part of God's moral perfection includes the fact that God cannot rightly approve what is not morally perfect. If a local judge were to sit on the bench in your county courthouse and spend all afternoon applauding the infractions and crimes of everyone who came before him, you'd be quick to sign his recall petition. A good person cannot be a bad or unjust judge. In God's instructions to the earthly judges in Israel, he uses himself as the standard: *"You shall not pervert the justice due to your poor in his lawsuit... I will not acquit the wicked. And you shall take no bribe, for a bribe blinds the clear-sighted and subverts the cause of those who are in the right"* (Ex.23:6-8).

This is clearly the most unpleasant aspect of what we learn about God in the Bible – unpleasant only because we contemplate his justice from the perspective of the guilty. It is hard to imagine a guilty criminal being excited about the absolutely perfect justice of the earthly judge he is scheduled to face. And so it has been hard for people throughout history to rightly and accurately affirm that God is just – perfectly just.

These are the parts of the Bible we tend to avoid. But we must not. Before we ever contemplate God's amazing grace that allows us to be made right with him, we have to consider the exacting justice of our Creator. He demonstrates this justice throughout the pages of the Bible. Consider the chilling words of Nahum 1:2-8.

> *The Lord is a jealous and avenging God; the Lord is avenging and wrathful; the Lord takes vengeance on his adversaries and keeps wrath for his enemies. The Lord is slow to anger and great in power, and the Lord will by no means clear the guilty. His way is in whirlwind and storm, and the clouds are the dust of his feet. He rebukes the sea and makes it dry; he dries up all the rivers; Bashan and Carmel wither; the bloom of Lebanon withers. The mountains quake before him; the hills melt; the earth heaves before him, the world and all who dwell in it. Who can stand before his indignation? Who can endure the heat of his anger? His*

> wrath is poured out like fire, and the rocks
> are broken into pieces by him. The LORD is
> good, a stronghold in the day of trouble;
> he knows those who take refuge in him. But
> with an overflowing flood he will make a
> complete end of the adversaries, and will
> pursue his enemies into darkness.

As unpleasant as it is to consider, the truth about the God of the Bible is that he is a just God who, because of his moral perfection, must respond in exacting justice to sin and evil. He responds not according to our relativistic standards and sliding scales, but according to his perfect and absolute standards. All infractions and transgressions must be accounted for. Because he is holy and just and because he is our Creator, he must judge us.

Don't fall to the myth that this kind of justice is a throwback remnant of the bloody Old Testament times. God is immutable and unchanging. While his redemptive plan does unfold as the biblical centuries roll by, his nature and character do not change or evolve. God is as just today as he was when he described his justice through the pen of Nahum in the seventh century BC. Consider these New Testament descriptions of God's exacting justice:

> And he commanded us to preach to the
> people and to testify that he is the one
> appointed by God to be judge of the living

and the dead. *(Ac.10:42)*

But because of your hard and impenitent heart you are storing up wrath for yourself on the day of wrath when God's righteous judgment will be revealed. He will render to each one according to his works. (Rom.2:5-6)

So it will be at the close of the age. The angels will come out and separate the evil from the righteous and throw them into the fiery furnace. In that place there will be weeping and gnashing of teeth.
(Mt.13:49-50)

[God] commands all people everywhere to repent, because he has fixed a day on which he will judge the world in righteousness by a man whom he has appointed; and of this he has given assurance to all by raising him from the dead. (Ac.17:30-31)

Then I saw heaven opened, and behold, a white horse! The one sitting on it is called Faithful and True, and in righteousness he judges and makes war. His eyes are like a flame of fire, and on his head are many diadems, and he has a name written that no one knows but himself. He is clothed in a robe dipped in blood, and the name by which he is called is The Word of God. And the armies of heaven, arrayed in fine linen, white and pure, were following him on white horses. From his mouth comes a sharp sword with which to strike down the nations, and he will rule them with a rod of iron. He will tread the winepress of the fury of the wrath of God the Almighty. (Rev.19:11-15)

Obviously the justice of God is still biblically vogue, though it's full vent may be scheduled for a future date. God is a God who because he is our Creator and because he is just will (and does) respond in judgment to sin. I say "does," because many of the things which currently happen in this world are expressions of God's justice. Consider the words of Psalm 7:11 that remind us that *"God is a righteous judge, and a God who feels indignation every day."* He not only feels it, he expresses it often according to various Old Testament and New Testament accounts.[7]

Contemplating the justice of God leaves us in a quandary. We know we must give an account to God, because he is our Creator. We know his standard is perfection because he's holy, and we're not. We then read of his absolute justice and begin to realize the insurmountable problem we face. The full and complete justice of God seems inevitable for us. Enter our only hope: God is also loving!

---

[7] See 1 Chronicles 13:10 and Acts 5:1-11.

God is Loving

Were it not for the incredible and incomparable love of God, we could have ended the biblical story in three chapters: God creates, people rebel, God assigns sinners to a place of exacting judgment. But that is not how the story ends. One thousand, one hundred and eighty-six chapters follow the first three, and in these God unfolds the story of his redemptive love.

We should stop for a moment and consider what the Bible does not mean by the word "love." Biblical love is not an emotional or affable feeling. Divine love is not cast as a romantic response to a sense of attraction. Actually, God's love couldn't be more of a contrast. God loves rebellious sinners not because there is something lovable or attractive about them. And certainly at the apex of his redemptive love, when Christ is provided as an excruciating and painful payment for our debt, there is hardly a good feeling present. God's love is hardly the sappy, sentimental, emotional concept that so many today tend to think it is.

God's love is a purposeful and intentional plan to benefit us for his glory and our undeserved good. God looked at the lost and hopeless situation we created for ourselves and then worked at great cost to himself, to do something to reverse it. God's love is undoubtedly the theme and treasure of everyone who has been eternally and profoundly benefited by it, but it should never be translated or redefined into a sweet, romantic love story. Those of us who have been made right before God's tribunal by his undeserved love, understand it as something far too profound and weighty for that.

From God's redemptive love flow words like "grace," mercy" and "kindness." Consider this amazingly rich prelude to one of the most familiar passages in the New Testament.

> *And you were dead in the trespasses and sins in which you once walked, following the course of this world, following the prince of the power of the air, the spirit that is now at work in the sons of disobedience— among whom we all once lived in the passions of our flesh, carrying out the desires of the body and the mind, and were by nature children of wrath, like the rest of mankind. But God, being rich in mercy, because of the great love with which he loved us, even when we were dead in our trespasses, made us alive together with Christ—by grace you have been saved— and raised us up with him and seated us with him in the heavenly places in Christ Jesus, so that in the coming ages he might show the immeasurable riches of his grace in kindness toward us in Christ Jesus. (Eph.2:1-7)*

God's love is great because of what it accomplished through Christ for our good and his own glory. It's not the kind of love that inspires us to jump up and high-five our beloved sidekick, but it is the kind of love that leads us in humility to bow down before a sacrificial and holy Redeemer. This is the current scene in heaven according to Revelation 5:8-9 which speaks of the inhabitants who "fell down before the Lamb... and they sang a new song, saying, 'Worthy are you to take the scroll and to open its seals, for you were slain, and by your blood you ransomed people for God from every tribe and language and people and nation."

Getting right with God starts with affirming the basic attributes of God – he is our Creator, he is holy, he is just and thankfully he is also extraordinarily loving. Some don't prefer to see God this way. But if the Bible is God's word, then this is the only God there is – Creator, holy, just and loving. And out of his great love he has mercifully provided the mechanism by which we can be freed from our ultimate problem and made right before him.

Chapter 2
The Bad News

The word "gospel" means "good news." It is the term God chose to describe the message that delineates how we can be freed from the penalty of our sins and restored one day to an ultimate place of blessing and righteousness. It is clearly very good news. But all of that good news is predicated on our acceptance of the bad news concerning ourselves and our current situation.

Good News without Bad News?

There is probably no other singular problem as glaring in today's retelling (or should I say contorting) of God's message of the gospel as people talking about God's "good news" without any mention of the biblical "bad news." Often times well-meaning churchgoers want to share a "positive message" about the "wonderful things" God wants to give, but the foundational reasons and problems that the gospel was given to solve are absent from their explanations. This leaves people without any truthful reference point for words like "saved" or "salvation."

A batch of poorly trained, but well-intentioned missionary candidates were once asked, "What are you going out to 'save' people from?" Their answers revealed their deficient theology. Some stated, "We want to save people from loneliness." Others said, "We want to save people from purposelessness," and some explained, "We want to see people saved from depression and broken-heartedness." That sounds like fine social work, but it in no way resembles the gospel of Jesus Christ. Good news without bad news reduces the message of the Bible to some kind of "life-improvement" program or "life-coaching" method. (And not a particularly great one, as we will address later.)

Often today's evangelistic methods and "calls to Christ" imply this perspective. They are presented with appeals like "Do you want a better life?" or "Would you like to find meaning and purpose in life?" They usually start with a proclamation of God's love and leave God's holiness and justice to the fine print, if they appear in the presentation at all.

Entreaties to "be saved" start to sound like one junior high boy telling another, "Susie loves you!" To which the other might respond, "Who's Susie?" "What does she look like?" "Do you really think I'll like her?" The pitch might eventually get reduced to "Give her a try!" "Who knows you might like her." And who hasn't seen the "Try God" bumper stickers? Are we really attempting to get people to "give God a whirl" because "he really loves them" and "he's really a delightful Person who will do some pretty nifty things for them"? Nothing could be further from the truth of what we find in the Bible regarding the call of Christ.

The biblical gospel is a solution to a problem – an urgent problem – a problem that every one of us has. It is the problem we need to see, admit and personally embrace!

Trying to Ignore the Problem

We all naturally tend to ignore the problem of sin, guilt and culpability before God, or at least we prefer to see it as someone else's problem. We do this because admitting the problem would have grave and unsettling ramifications. If we really accepted the biblical diagnosis that we don't measure up to our Creator's standards and that because of his perfect nature he must exact punishment on sinners like us, it would be upsetting to say the least. Who of us could live peacefully knowing that every day our compromised thoughts, attitudes and conduct are storing up for us more and more condemnation for when we meet our Maker?

The biggest diversion is to periodically fixate on others who are "bigger sinners" than we are and to hope that our relative sense of righteousness will somehow safeguard us from God's punishment. The Apostle Paul describes this strategy in his letter to the Romans.

> *Therefore you have no excuse, O man, every one of you who judges. For in passing judgment on another you condemn yourself,*

> *because you, the judge, practice the very
> same things. We know that the judgment of
> God rightly falls on those who practice such
> things. Do you suppose, O man—you who
> judge those who practice such things and yet
> do them yourself—that you will escape the
> judgment of God? (Romans 2:1-3)*

Paul is arguing that if we discern and condemn error in others, we prove we have the ability to recognize sin for what it is. Our problem is the stubborn refusal to turn that same discerning evaluation toward ourselves and to identify and admit our own errors. We show a kind of exacting judgment in our evaluation of others, but we selfishly give ourselves a pass.

This propensity is easy to see as we drive in traffic. When someone cuts in front of our vehicle we are quick to discern and condemn the other person's driving errors, citing traffic laws, asking, "Where's a cop when you need him?" and perhaps even uttering a few disparaging adjectives regarding the driver's lack of intelligence. But when the horn honks at us and we realize we've cut someone off on the road, it is amazing how none of our exacting judgments are turned on ourselves. We are quick with excuses and reasons for our poor lane changes, sometimes going so far as to disparage the "uptight" drivers and "hotheads" who like to overuse their horns.

Watching the evening news or reading the crime

blotter doesn't help our objectivity either. It is easy to write off the "dregs of society" highlighted on the newscast and bolster our sense of superiority, even beginning to believe that our sins are hardly sins at all, I mean, we didn't murder anybody or rob a bank.

Jesus spent a considerable amount of time demonstrating that our sins may be different by degree from that notorious sinner we despise, but when it comes to categorically different, they really aren't. Jesus taught:

> *"You have heard that it was said to those of old, 'You shall not murder; and whoever murders will be liable to judgment.' But I say to you that everyone who is angry with his brother will be liable to judgment; whoever insults his brother will be liable to the council; and whoever says, 'You fool!' will be liable to the hell of fire." (Matthew 5:21-22)*

Jesus went on to teach:

> *"You have heard that it was said, 'You shall not commit adultery.' But I say to you that everyone who looks at a woman with lustful intent has already committed adultery with her in his heart." (Matthew 5:27-28)*

Of course angrily calling a person a disparaging name is different than killing him, but you have to admit they are categorically similar – the same sinful hatred fuels them both. Likewise, indulging your mind with lustful thoughts of a woman who is not your wife is not the same as sleeping with her, but the thoughts are not really in a different category, are they? They are both motivated by the same illicit appetites.

Jesus wants us to see and admit that our sins are sins, regardless of how extensively we have expressed them. He wants us to see that our hearts are sinful and rebellious against his perfect moral mandates. Can you admit that you are sinful? Do you see that your heart is not in sync with the holy standards of God? Will you readily confess, without providing excuses, that you do not measure up to the righteous requirements of God's rules?

Personally Embracing the Problem

We must not ignore or rationalize our problem, but rather embrace it – admit it, own it, and agree with God that his diagnosis is true. That's what the word "confess" means. To "confess our sins" means that we are agreeing with God's evaluation and assessment of our thoughts, attitudes and behaviors. It is not looking at our lives through our own lens of relative goodness or comparative superiority. Confession requires that we see ourselves objectively, from God's holy and righteous perspective. This is why any presentation of the gospel must begin with a clear and accurate perspective of who God is. If we do not see him as perfectly holy and just, we will likely not see our real problem. After all, comparatively speaking, we all know "worse sinners" than ourselves.

A classic example of this kind of objective evaluation is found in Isaiah 6. King Uzziah had just died, ending a long and prosperous chapter in Judah's history. Unfortunately, as in most prosperous periods of a society, affluence and success had lulled the nation into thinking less of God's righteousness and impeccable holiness. Part of God's remedy was to give the prophet Isaiah an unvarnished glimpse into how holy he actually is. Isaiah records the scene:

> In the year that King Uzziah died I saw the Lord sitting upon a throne, high and lifted up; and the train of his robe filled the temple. Above him stood the seraphim. Each had six wings: with two he covered his face, and with two he covered his feet, and with two he flew. And one called to another and said: "Holy, holy, holy is the LORD of hosts; the whole earth is full of his glory!" And the foundations of the thresholds shook at the voice of him who called, and the house was filled with smoke. (Isaiah 6:1-4)

This was to be a catalytic event for Isaiah's ministry. It's not that Isaiah hadn't seen the sin in his morally lax culture. He had. For the five chapters leading up to this event we read of Isaiah delivering resounding indictments on the compromised ethics and deplorable acts of the sinful society he lived in. Much like the evening news or the newspaper's crime blotter, those sins were overt and obvious to anyone who had read of God's commands and precepts. But in light of this revelatory encounter in God's throne room Isaiah responds with this personal and contrite outburst:

> And I said: "Woe is me! For I am lost; for I
> am a man of unclean lips, and I dwell in the
> midst of a people of unclean lips; for my eyes
> have seen the King, the LORD of hosts!"
> (Isaiah 6:5)

Rightly perceiving the flawless character and majesty of God, Isaiah was concerned about something as seemingly small and insignificant as the way he spoke and the words he chose to use. Now sin was his problem as well as a problem for everyone in his culture. God is so holy and so perfectly righteous, that with a clear perception of the authority of our Creator, the One to whom we must all give an account, no one can "feel okay" about their moral performance or their ethical track record. As the Bible repeatedly states:

> No one living is righteous before you.
> (Psalm 143:2)

Who can say, "I have made my heart pure; I am clean from my sin"? (Proverbs 20:9)

What is man, that he can be pure? Or he who is born of a woman, that he can be righteous? (Job 15:14)

There is no one who does not sin (1 Kings 8:46)

All our righteous deeds are like a polluted garment. (Isaiah 64:6)

If we say we have no sin, we deceive ourselves, and the truth is not in us. (1 John 1:8)

For all have sinned and fall short of the glory of God. (Romans 3:23)

This is God's truthful assessment of us from his holy vantage point. And it needs to be ours. We cannot solve the problem without owning up to our sin. No more rationalization and no more making up excuses. There may be reasons for our sins, but the Bible requires that we come to God without excuses. Sometimes it is easier to admit our sin when we end up as a "dreg" on the evening news. But even if we don't, we must all admit that we have a sin problem.

Two Sinners

Consider the story Jesus told in Luke 18 about two men who went up to the temple to pray, one a religious leader and the other a societal outcast. The religious leader spent his prayer time feeling good about his moral resumé as it compared with the dregs of his day. The outcast owned up to his moral bankruptcy, confessed it and humbly pleaded with God for mercy. His prayer didn't sound anything like the religious leader's. It hardly seemed to be a prayer at all. It was a contrite, heartfelt expression to his holy Creator as to just how sinful he understood himself to be. Here's Jesus' comment on his own story: "*I tell you, this man* [the dreg] *went down to his house justified, rather than the other* [the religious leader]" (Luke 18:14).

The word "justified" is such an important word in the Bible. It is a legal word that speaks to the release of the penalty associated with our spiritual crimes and moral transgressions. It is a more powerful and complete expression of the concept of "forgiveness." And this word is often used to describe what happens when God solves our problem.

So Jesus' commentary clarifies that no matter how righteous we may think we are compared to the next guy, we will not be forgiven of the sins which in fact exist before our holy Creator unless we admit, own, and concede that we are guilty before God.

So enough of the comparisons, no longer can

we rationalize the "small sins" because they are not "big sins." The folly of this is much like one skunk feeling good about himself because he doesn't smell as bad as the "really stinky" skunks. To humans they all smell bad. And to God we are all sinners. No use comparing the "stinkiness" of our transgressions. We all stink before a perfectly righteous God. The good news is, God has provided a way to remove all of our sin, but the key is to admit our sin to him.

Scales on Judgment Day?

If pressed, most people will admit to the presence of some moral failure or character flaw in their lives. But they usually suggest a solution to those demerits by expressing a belief that their "good behavior" must in some way cancel out the bad. Most of the world's religions and every aberration of Christianity teach exactly that. Your supposed "good deeds" will mitigate or obliterate any consequence for your so-called "bad deeds." Our future reckoning with our Creator is depicted as involving some set of celestial scales on which each person's deeds are weighed and those who receive a divine "pass" are those whose "good" outweighs their "bad."

But that is not what Jesus taught and it certainly isn't what the Bible tells us. Remember Jesus' words to the "dreg of society" in Luke 18? If one's "good deeds" were capable of counterbalancing one's "bad deeds," then we would expect Jesus to share this life-giving news! He might have said something like, "To be justified this man now needs to step-up his performance of good deeds so that they can begin to outnumber his bad ones." But this is not what Jesus said. The man's "justification" wasn't to be accomplished in the future, there was no prescription to start "out-weighing" all the bad, the forgiveness Jesus spoke of was immediate and not based on some set of moral scales.

The Bible couldn't be clearer on this point and yet the average person, both inside and outside of the church, seems quick to default to this false paradigm - that your "good" can cancel out your "bad." This global misperception must be one of the reasons God ordained that Jesus would affirm the justification of a notorious sinner on his proverbial "deathbed." Think back to the familiar scene at Christ's crucifixion, as Jesus hung between two criminals. One of them continued to be crass, hardened and obstinate. The other was contrite, penitent and softhearted toward Christ. To him, Jesus said, *"Today you will be with me in Paradise"* (Luke 23:43). This is a fatal blow to the "scale theory" of justification. He had no time to make up for his criminal life of bad deeds. There was no opportunity for any good deeds to cancel out his bad. But as boldly as Jesus declared the Luke 18 dreg to be "justified," so here Jesus declares that on his final day this felonious man is guaranteed forgiveness when he faces his Maker.

Don't let this ubiquitous lie ever find a place in

your thinking. Getting right with God, having your sins cancelled out, has nothing to do with a set of "make-up assignments" or a road map of good deeds, or a set of heavenly scales. Sins are forgiven as we accept responsibility for them and trust in the good news of the gospel and the saving work of Christ.

A Two-Part Problem

While we often talk about sin as a problem in our behavior (which it certainly is), there is actually more to the story. The Bible tells us that our sinful attitudes and actions are really a symptom of our sinful standing before God – or should I say "separation" before God.

It is a popular misconception to think that we are all born spiritually and morally innocent, and that as we grow old enough to distinguish right and wrong, that then we are found guilty and actually become sinful. But the Bible repeatedly tells us that our problem with sin actually began before we were born – not in terms of our personal acts of sin, but as it relates to our state or position of separation. That's an important distinction! "Sin" is not only a description of our actions; it is also a description of our state of being or our position before God.

Remember that Adam and Eve initially destroyed their relationship with God by disobeying him. The Bible describes our first parents' sins as impacting not only themselves, but also the children they produced. Each subsequent generation of the human race was thereafter born into a state of separation from God. The "garden test" of choosing good or evil, with the resultant consequence of separation from God was not repeated in every generation. Consider biological death, which was said to be one of the results of Adam and Eve's sin. Death affected not only Adam, but also all of Adam's offspring even before they would each make a conscious, moral choice to do what was right or wrong. If this were not the case, then young children would be impervious to death until they reached an age of making thoughtful sinful choices.

While this fact may raise a series of important questions, (some that the Bible addresses and others that the Bible does not explicitly address), it is a helpful truth that allows us to make sense of the reality in which we live. Each person since Adam is "born in sin" – that is, in a state of separation from God (cf. Ps.51:5). It was a problem "gifted" to us just by being born as human beings. On the flip side, as Romans 5:12-21 clarifies, we can gain a position of complete forgiveness and righteousness "gifted" to us through Christ. More on this later, but realize that this is one of the reasons why the "scales on Judgment Day" theory is wrong. Those associated with Christ have been "gifted" a right relationship with God, just as those formally associated with Adam have had the wrong relationship with God "gifted" to them through Adam.

This wrong relationship of "separation" is the reason everyone is born naturally sinning and choosing to put themselves and their own agendas before God and his agenda. Another way to describe this separation is "death"—not biological, but relational. Read carefully these words from the New Testament:

> *And you were dead in the trespasses and*
> *sins in which you once walked, following the*
> *course of this world, following the prince of*
> *the power of the air, the spirit that is now at*
> *work in the sons of disobedience—among*
> *whom we all once lived in the passions of our*
> *flesh, carrying out the desires of the body*
> *and the mind, and were by nature children of*
> *wrath, like the rest of mankind.*
> *(Ephesians 2:1-3)*

As this passage makes clear, even though our sinful actions may be a natural outgrowth of our sinful position (living as "dead" to God), our individual sinful actions are still punishable before God. We may have an inborn bent to sin, but when we consciously make sinful choices we are culpable, guilty and liable for each conscious sinful act. That is, unless of course, we individually cling to Christ and have the gift of a right relationship with God "gifted" to us. As Romans 2 tells us:

*We know that the judgment of God rightly
falls on those who practice such things. Do
you suppose, O man—you who judge those
who practice such things and yet do them
yourself—that you will escape the judgment
of God? Or do you presume on the riches
of his kindness and forbearance and
patience, not knowing that God's kindness
is meant to lead you to repentance? But
because of your hard and impenitent heart
you are storing up wrath for yourself on the
day of wrath when God's righteous judgment
will be revealed. (Romans 2:2-5)*

We must understand that regardless of our stage
of life, or our degree of wicked transgressions we
are all in need of getting it right with God – having
our status changed from "separated" to "reconciled."
Because those who die separated from God are left
to face a day of exacting judgment regarding each
conscious sinful action, while those reconciled to God
through Christ have the assurance of a full acquittal
and an unearned exoneration.

The Bible explains that our existence in one of
two eternal places is based on who we are associated
with – Adam or Christ. And one's experience in either
of those eternal abodes is said to be based on our
conscious acts of obedience or disobedience. In other
words, the experience in the place of judgment or in
the New Jerusalem will not be same for everyone.

There are certainly degrees of retribution and degrees of reward (see Rom.2:12-16; Rev.20:11-12; 2Cor.5:10; Mt.6:19-21).

The question of those born "in Adam" who die without ever reaching a place of moral consciousness and obviously never becoming capable of volitionally being "in Christ" is a sticking point for many and the reason lots of people ignore or deny the biblical data regarding our inborn position of separation before God. It is a topic for another book in which one would seek to lay out some biblical logic and theological extrapolation, because God doesn't explicitly address the issue in his word. But suffice it to say that God is perfectly just and abundantly kind, and his provision of grace and his divine decision to associate such people with Christ is expectantly anticipated.

But that of course is not the situation for those who are reading these words. And such mysterious and thought-provoking questions should never impede the mature and morally conscious person from pondering the predicament of their own situation and seeking God's solution.

God's Work in Getting Us to See Our Sin

Perhaps your endurance to still be reading these poignant sentences about our problem is a positive sign that God is at work in your life in order to bring you to see the problem as your own. The Bible tells us that God has positioned things in each person's life so that "*they should seek God, in the hope that they might feel their way toward him and find him*" (Ac.17:26-27). This reconciliation cannot take place without a conviction and ownership of our sinful situation and compounding sinful actions. Thankfully God does not leave us to our own devices and efforts. God sends his Spirit for that very purpose. Jesus said,

> *Nevertheless, I tell you the truth: it is to your advantage that I go away, for if I do not go away, the Helper will not come to you. But if I go, I will send him to you. And when he comes, he will convict the world concerning sin and righteousness and judgment:*
> *(John 16:7-8)*

God is at work in people around the world bringing them to conviction concerning their problem, showing them how they fall short of God's standards by the ways in which they sin against God, and warning them of the pending consequences for their transgressions. That is the foundational work of God in the lives of individuals he is bringing to himself. When you sense the pangs of conviction regarding your problem, know it is a necessary starting point. It should lead you to explore and appropriate God's solution to your dilemma, which is found in Christ.

This conviction that God's Spirit works in our lives is always more than a mental assent, it is a kind of contrition and shame as we saw in Isaiah when he stood before his Creator and said *"Woe to me! For I am lost!"* (Is.6:5). It is a kind of admission that recognizes that there is nothing in us that is worthy of acceptance before God. It is a brokenness that realizes that we are not only sinful, but worthy of God's specific and exacting punishment.

If you don't have it, pray for it. Ask God to show you the predicament of sin and the consequences of your fallen state. Ask for the clarity David had in Psalm 51.

> *For I know my transgressions, and my sin is*
> *ever before me. Against you, you only, have I*
> *sinned and done what is evil in your sight,*
> *so that you may be justified in your words*
> *and blameless in your judgment. Behold,*
> *I was brought forth in iniquity, and in sin did*
> *my mother conceive me. (Psalm 51:3-5)*

If there is no ownership of your sin problem, then the following pages are merely academic. But if your heart and emotions have been seized by the perilous position you are in before a holy God because of your sin, then the following chapters will be full of life-changing words that will map out God's message of reconciliation – the good news of Jesus Christ.

"And there is salvation in no one else, for there is no other name under heaven given among men by which we must be saved."

Acts 4:12

Chapter 3
The Good News: Jesus Christ

Jesus is the "good news." The Bible presents him as the solution for our ultimate problem. He accomplished for us what we were unable to do for ourselves. He is presented not as our helper or assistant, but as the final and complete solution to our sin problem. Jesus Christ is the focal point of the gospel and the focal point of the Bible. The emphasis on Christ cannot be overstated.

Jesus himself made it clear that we cannot get things right with our Creator until we deal with who he is and what he has done. He stated it as clearly as it could be said: *"I am the way, and the truth, and the life. No one comes to the Father except through me"* (John 14:6).

Who is Jesus?

This is a question that demands an answer. Given the massive impact Jesus has made in history, he is a difficult figure to ignore. People have been forced to formulate an opinion of who this person is and what the events of his life mean. Even Jesus pressed this question when he turned to his disciples and asked, *"Who do you say that I am?"* (Mt.16:13-15). As others have rightly pointed out, you can either write him off as crazy, or say that he was a charlatan pitching some enormous lies about himself, or you can agree with his claims regarding his extraordinary life. What you can't do is create an imaginary hybrid of a nice Jesus who just wanted to leave behind some moral instructions. His claims are too extreme for that.[1]

Back to the question. According to Jesus, Peter answered correctly when he said, *"You are the Christ, the Son of the living God"* (Mt.16:16). To say "the Christ" was to say that Jesus was the fulfillment of all the Old Testament expectations. "Christ" is the Greek word for "Messiah." Messiah means "the Anointed One." Anointing was the Jewish act of ceremonially pouring oil on the head of one who was being inaugurated as either a prophet (1Kgs.19:16), priest (Ex.30:30) or king (1Sam.16:13). Israel's prophets spoke for God, Israel's priests represented the people to God and Israel's kings governed the people on behalf of God.

While there were a few highpoints within the Old Testament history of the prophets, priests and kings, the Bible was clear that the ultimate One was still coming. He was to be more than an imperfect human filling these roles for only a generation. An eternal,

---

[1] Again, this is often side-stepped by saying that the records of Christ's claims in the Gospels of Matthew, Mark, Luke and John are somehow inaccurate or corrupted. This is such a common fallback claim that few skeptics even bother to question its veracity. But you should. See C.E. Hill's *Who Chose the Gospels: Probing the Great Gospel Conspiracy* (Oxford Press, 2010) or Darrell Bock's *The Missing Gospels: Unearthing the Truth behind Alternative Christianities* (Thomas Nelson, 2006).

perfect and everlasting "Christ" was coming, who was to perfectly and completely fulfill these roles, that is, One who perfectly spoke for God, perfectly represented the people to God and perfectly governed the people for God.

Because all human beings are sinful, imperfect and subject to death, God became a man and perfectly fulfilled these roles himself. This is where the second half of Peter's answer comes in. Jesus is *"the Son of the living God"* (Mt.16:17).

Jesus is God

Jesus' claim to be "the Son of the living God" is the summation of all of the "ultimate Son" prophecies in the Old Testament. Here are a few of the more familiar ones we often hear quoted around Christmastime:

> *Therefore the Lord himself will give you a sign. Behold, the virgin shall conceive and bear a son, and shall call his name Immanuel. (Isaiah 7:14)*

> *For to us a child is born, to us a son is given; and the government shall be upon his shoulder, and his name shall be called Wonderful Counselor, Mighty God, Everlasting Father, Prince of Peace. Of the increase of his government and of peace there will be no end, on the throne of David*

*and over his kingdom, to establish it and to
uphold it with justice and with righteousness
from this time forth and forevermore. The
zeal of the L*ORD *of hosts will do this.
(Isaiah 9:6-7)*

*But you, O Bethlehem Ephrathah, who are
too little to be among the clans of Judah,
from you shall come forth for me one who is
to be ruler in Israel, whose coming forth is
from of old, from ancient days. (Micah 5:2)*

We can assume that these passages were among
the many that Jesus pointed to when showing the
connection between his life and the prophecies of the
Old Testament regarding the "ultimate Son." Consider
the account of the "impromptu Bible study" in Luke
24, where Jesus chided those who were *"slow of
heart to believe all that the prophets have spoken···
And beginning with Moses and all the Prophets, he
interpreted to them in all the Scriptures the things
concerning himself"* (Lk.24:25-27).

The disciples got the message. They recognized
that only God could accomplish what was needed
to solve our ultimate problem. Read this extended
introduction to John's Gospel carefully. Notice the
complex nature of the Triune God, which undergirds
the message of God taking on humanity to solve our
sin problem.

*In the beginning was the Word, and the
Word was with God, and the Word was God.
He was in the beginning with God. All things
were made through him, and without him
was not any thing made that was made. In
him was life, and the life was the light of men.
The light shines in the darkness, and the
darkness has not overcome it. There was a
man sent from God, whose name was John.
He came as a witness, to bear witness about
the light, that all might believe through him.
He was not the light, but came to bear witness
about the light. The true light, which
enlightens everyone, was coming into the
world. He was in the world, and the world
was made through him, yet the world did not
know him. He came to his own, and his own
people did not receive him. But to all who did
receive him, who believed in his name, he
gave the right to become children of God,
who were born, not of blood nor of the will
of the flesh nor of the will of man, but of God.
And the Word became flesh and dwelt among
us, and we have seen his glory, glory as of
the only Son from the Father, full of grace
and truth. (John bore witness about him, and
cried out, "This was he of whom I said, 'He
who comes after me ranks before me,
because he was before me.'") And from his
fullness we have all received, grace upon*

grace. For the law was given through Moses; grace and truth came through Jesus Christ. No one has ever seen God; the only God, who is at the Father's side, he has made him known. (John 1:1-18)

The tri-unity of God may be difficult for us to come to terms with because we are not accustomed to reconciling the reality of three distinct Persons existing as one essence. But that is how the real God is presented to us in Scripture. According to the Bible "God is one" and there is in fact only "one God" and yet the Father is God, the Son is God, and the Spirit is God - all at the same time. The "personhood" of each does not overlap and is not modal in that the Father is not the Son, the Spirit is not the Father, nor is Jesus the Spirit. While growing intellectually comfortable with this complexity may necessitate more contemplation, we should all concede that a complex and inscrutable Deity is to be expected if he is to be real.[2]

The rest of the New Testament continues to affirm this seemingly incomprehensible reality – that God became a man to permanently solve our sin problem.

---

[2] For more biblical basics on the Trinity or the "Tri-unity" of God see introductions like Millard Erickson's *Making Sense of the Trinity: Three Crucial Questions* (Baker Books, 2000) or Robert Bowman's *Why You Should Believe in the Trinity* (Baker Books, 1989). For a more thorough and historical survey try works like Robert Letham's *The Holy Trinity: In Scripture, History, Theology and Worship* (P & R Publishing, 2005) or James White's *The Forgotten Trinity: Recovering the Heart of Christian Belief* (Bethany House, 1998).

But why didn't God solve this problem from heaven? Why did divinity have to take on humanity and live among us?

Why God Became a Man

It is hard to find a Bible passage that speaks of the incarnation without also mentioning a connection to the incarnate Christ's death. We are reminded in passage after passage that we should always see Jerusalem's cross from Bethlehem's stable. God, according to Scripture, became a man because man needed to be redeemed by "human currency." The wages of human sin is human death and divine punishment against human beings. The Father sends the Son as a true human being to absorb the Father's wrath against humanity and satisfy divine justice against real human beings.

Consider the following prophetic description of this redemptive work in Isaiah's prophecy regarding the incarnate Lamb of God, given some six centuries before Christ was born in Bethlehem. While the prophecy begins in a future tense, God quickly shifts in his descriptions to what some have called the "prophetic perfect" – a grammatical tense that portrays events as already accomplished. This is a stylistic device that God uses from time to time which, among other things, reveals the certainty with which God purposes to bring the described things about. And of course he did, some six centuries later as recorded in the New Testament.

Isaiah 52:13 begins, *"Behold, my servant shall act wisely; he shall be high and lifted up, and shall be exalted" this is an interesting way to describe this Servant because Isaiah had previously described the one God of Israel to be "high, lifted up and exalted"* (Is.6:1; 33:5; 40:26). This is obviously no ordinary servant.

Immediately, Isaiah 52:14 moves from what you might expect regarding the Father's exalted Servant to say, *"As many were astonished at you— his appearance was so marred, beyond human semblance, and his form beyond that of the children of mankind."* We are not introduced here to images of a regal, reigning Messiah, but to a suffering Christ who is brutally slain and beaten.

The next verse, Isaiah 52:15, tells us why: *"so shall he sprinkle many nations."* The Levitical image of the priest "sprinkling" with hyssop plant branches dipped in blood, would come to mind for the Jewish audience. The sprinkling symbolized the cleansing of sin. This symbolic picture and its colors were alluded to in the first chapter of Isaiah when he wrote, *"though your sins are like scarlet, they shall be as white as snow; though they are red like crimson, they shall become like wool"* (Is.1:18). In this case, the cleansing would not be just for Israel or for those who came under the jurisdiction of the Levites, but for *"many nations;"* this has in view the fruition of God's promise to Abraham (*"in you all the families of the earth will be blessed"* – Gen.12:3b).

Isaiah 53 goes on to describe the sacrifice of this Suffering Servant and the associated benefits. Look for the verses that allude to the Suffering Servant's life after death. Notice the recurring theme of the innocent receiving the penalty in the place of the guilty and the language of the Old Testament sacrificial system, where lambs were symbolically representative of the innocent. In this case, as biblical history made crystal clear, the innocent One was none other than the "Lamb of God," Jesus Christ, the incarnate eternal and holy One.

> *Surely he has borne our griefs*
> *and carried our sorrows;*
> *yet we esteemed him stricken,*
> *smitten by God, and afflicted.*
> *But he was wounded for our transgressions;*
> *he was crushed for our iniquities;*
> *upon him was the chastisement that*
> *brought us peace,*
> *and with his stripes we are healed.*
> *All we like sheep have gone astray;*
> *we have turned—every one—to his own way;*
> *and the* Lord *has laid on him*
> *the iniquity of us all.*
> *He was oppressed, and he was afflicted,*
> *yet he opened not his mouth;*
> *like a lamb that is led to the slaughter,*
> *and like a sheep that before its shearers is*
> *silent,*

so he opened not his mouth.
By oppression and judgment he was taken
*   away;*
and as for his generation, who considered
that he was cut off out of the land of the
*   living,*
stricken for the transgression of my people?
And they made his grave with the wicked
and with a rich man in his death,
although he had done no violence,
and there was no deceit in his mouth.
Yet it was the will of the Lord to crush him;
he has put him to grief;
when his soul makes an offering for guilt,
he shall see his offspring; he shall prolong
*   his days;*
the will of the Lord shall prosper in his
*   hand.*
Out of the anguish of his soul he shall see
*   and be satisfied;*
by his knowledge shall the righteous one,
*   my servant,*
make many to be accounted righteous,
and he shall bear their iniquities.
Therefore I will divide him a portion with
*   the many,*
and he shall divide the spoil with the strong,
because he poured out his soul to death
and was numbered with the transgressors;
yet he bore the sin of many, and makes

intercession for the transgressors.
(Isaiah 53:4–12)

Christ's Death

It is hard not to see the cross from the stable in a passage like Isaiah 53. Jesus became a human being to suffer and die so that we, sinful humans, could be "accounted righteous" through his substitutionary death. Because of his divinity we are provided a one time, eternally significant, human payment for sin, applicable to those who are not righteous, so as to provide us reconciliation and fellowship with our perfectly righteous Creator. Or in the words of 1 Peter 3:18, "Christ suffered once for sins, the righteous for the unrighteous, that he might bring us to God."

Notice too in Isaiah 53, that it speaks not only of the act of dying, but all the associated punishments that came with it. Christ's crucifixion was preceded by whipping, scourging and beatings, just to name a few of the forms of "chastisement" that God appointed for him (Is.53:5). Unlike today's forms of state execution, the Roman's method of crucifixion adopted from the Phoenicians, was not designed to simply kill a criminal, it was designed to torture him with a prolonged period of suffering and pain. This was not a "painless injection" to end his life, but rather it was a sustained conscious punishment, experienced so that he incurred what we deserve.

"The wages of sin is death" (Rom.6:23). And as

discussed in the second chapter, the "death" God sentenced on sinful mankind is more than physical. It is a kind of relational separation that includes a just and painful punishment for sinful actions. Jesus quoted Psalm 22:1 amid the painful suffering on the cross: *"My God, my God why have you forsaken me?"* (Mt.27:46). Christ recites the opening line of this familiar psalm, which foretells many aspects of the crucifixion, including the pain and the relational separation; he recites it not seeking an answer, but recites it as a statement of fact. In admittedly inconceivable terms, the Son expresses his experience of pain, punishment and separation from the Father. This is the experience we wholly deserve for all eternity. But the eternal Son experienced it in full force two thousand years ago, so that we would never have to.

Billions of earthly transgressions against a holy God were perfectly and completely paid for by a life with infinite value and intrinsic righteousness. With our sins atoned for by a righteous human substitute we can be delivered from sin's penalties. The sinless took the place of the sinful. As the New Testament states, *"For our sake he made him to be sin who knew no sin, so that in him we might become the righteousness of God"* (2Cor.5:21).

The Earthly Life of Jesus

To be made "the righteousness of God in him," or

to be counted as acceptable and holy because of our alliance with Christ, Jesus needed to not only die in our place, he needed to live in our place as well. Think about it, if Jesus' one assignment was to die for us, the Father could have sent the Son on the weekend of his crucifixion. Surely God could have orchestrated a very brief prelude to the scourging and execution of Jesus that would have satisfied divine justice. But instead we have Jesus born as an infant, weaned as a toddler, educated as a child, developed as an adolescent, and matured to be an adult. The Bible tells us that this was for a very important reason.

Christ told John the Baptist to baptize him in water with the symbolic baptism of repentance, even though there were no sins for which Christ was guilty. When John understandably tried to refuse by saying, *"I need to be baptized by you,"* Jesus responded by saying something critically important. Christ said, *"Let it be so now, for thus it is fitting for us to fulfill all righteousness"* (Mt.3:14-15). It was a "righteous" and obedient act to submit to the prophet John's command to be baptized in water as a sign of one's repentance. Though Christ himself had no need to do it because he had no need to repent of anything, there would be many who, for one reason or another, would fail to be baptized as they were instructed.

Think about the thief on the cross. He trusts in Christ, but the preponderance of his life to that point was full of crime, sin and immorality. Of course, we can assume that he had refused John's call to be baptized. So Jesus' human act of obedience, in this case to be baptized in water, could be accredited to the thief.

Imagine all the other acts of righteousness the thief failed to fulfill throughout his childhood, teenage years and adult life. Envision all the temptations and sins that the thief had fallen to over the years. He was in no way qualified to "enter paradise" as Jesus had promised (Lk.23:43). Even if his sins were blotted out, what about all the righteous requirements of the law that had been spelled out? Christ had lived them all out in that thief's place! He had fulfilled all the righteous requirements prescribed by the rules, ordinances and dictates of God. Jesus had victoriously said "no" to every temptation that the thief had said "yes" to. For the thief to trust in Christ on his dying day was to have the entirety of his life and all its associated misdeeds and negligence replaced and substituted for Christ's. This kind of transaction necessitated not only the payment for his misdeeds (i.e., Christ's death), but perfect success in doing all of the deeds God required (i.e., Christ's life). Jesus lived it all for him, from his childhood and all the way through his adult life.

This is the importance of Christ's earthly life. It was lived for all those who would put their trust in him. Paul summarizes both sides of this amazing transaction with these words:

There is therefore now no condemnation

*for those who are in Christ Jesus. For the law
of the Spirit of life has set you free in Christ
Jesus from the law of sin and death. For God
has done what the law, weakened by the
flesh, could not do. By sending his own Son
in the likeness of sinful flesh and for sin,
he condemned sin in the flesh, in order
that the righteous requirement of the law
might be fulfilled in us... (Romans 8:1-4a)*

The Resurrection of Christ

One of the great acts of Christ's ministry was to
*"deliver all those who through fear of death were
subject to lifelong slavery"* (Heb.2:14-15). Because
it is *"appointed for man to die once, and after that
comes the judgment"* (Heb.9:27), we intuitively and
rightly fear our appointment with death. Not only
is death loathed as an end to the common grace of
this life and the separation from loved ones, it is
also despised because it exposes the underlying fear
that we sinners have of facing our Day of reckoning.
While some may, by great effort *"suppress the truth"*
regarding that Day of judgment (Rom.1:18), most,
if they are honest, have a sense that the end of this
life may in fact initiate the beginning of the deserved
recompense regarding their sins.

But Christ's bodily resurrection from the dead
provides those who trust in him an abiding confidence
that the consequences of sin have been adequately

settled by the life and death of Christ. Remember that God clearly warned *"the wages of sin is death"* (Rom.6:23; Gen.2:17). Jesus Christ claims that his righteous life and his penalty-absorbing death have perfectly and completely paid the debt for us, thus cancelling all the eternal consequences. If Christ took care of the sin problem for us, we have confidence that he will take care of the death problem as well. That is what the physical resurrection of Christ testifies to. Not just the biological death problem, but the more serious relational or spiritual death problem that involves the retribution for our sins.

In one sense, the bodily resurrection of Jesus validates everything that the Bible claims about the Messiah from the beginning of Genesis to the end of Revelation. His claim to remove sin, his declaration to be God incarnate, the promise that he would be accounted as our righteousness, and the authority to call us all to trust in his "finished work," all these find their validation in the historic resurrection of Jesus Christ. As the opening lines of the Book of Romans state,

> *Paul, a servant of Christ Jesus, called to be an apostle, set apart for the gospel of God, which he promised beforehand through his prophets in the holy Scriptures, concerning his Son, who was descended from David according to the flesh and was declared to be the Son of God in power according to*

*the Spirit of holiness by his resurrection
from the dead, Jesus Christ our Lord, through
whom we have received grace and apostleship
to bring about the obedience of faith for the
sake of his name among all the nations,
including you who are called to belong to
Jesus Christ   (Romans 1:1-6)*

It may be impossible to overestimate the significance of the resurrection as evidence of Christ's claims and as assurance to us of Christ's redemptive work. This is why there is so much time allotted to Christ's resurrection in the apostolic preaching recorded in the Book of Acts. In a cursory reading of New Testament evangelism there is arguably more of an emphasis on Christ's resurrection than on any other single aspect of Christ's earthly ministry. That is not because his life and death are any less important, but rather because the eternal impact of his life and death are validated and verified by his resurrection. Our certain hope about our own future is predicated on the historicity of Jesus' resurrection. *"He has caused us to be born again to a living hope through the resurrection of Christ from the dead"* (1Pt.1:3). As Paul so boldly states, *"if Christ has not been raised, then our preaching is in vain and your faith is in vain... if Christ has not been raised, your faith is futile and you are still in your sins"* (1Cor.15:14, 17).

The central importance of the resurrection is one

reason that Jesus often spoke of his resurrection before it happened. Consider these verses from the gospel of Matthew, which are just a sampling of Jesus' promises regarding his resurrection.

> From that time Jesus began to show his disciples that he must go to Jerusalem and suffer many things from the elders and chief priests and scribes, and be killed, and on the third day be raised.(Mt.16:21)

> As they were gathering in Galilee, Jesus said to them, "The Son of Man is about to be delivered into the hands of men, and they will kill him, and he will be raised on the third day." And they were greatly distressed. (Mt.17:22-23)

> And as Jesus was going up to Jerusalem, he took the twelve disciples aside, and on the way he said to them, "See, we are going up to Jerusalem. And the Son of Man will be delivered over to the chief priests and scribes, and they will condemn him to death and deliver him over to the Gentiles to be mocked and flogged and crucified, and he will be raised on the third day." (Mt.20:17-19)

> "But after I am raised up, I will go before you to Galilee." (Mt.26:32)

It is hypocritical for "liberal Christians" who disdain talk of Jesus' literal resurrection to have any hope of their own resurrection. How can they, because of an anti-supernatural bias, dismiss talk of the literal, historical resurrection of Jesus and yet anticipate forgiveness, acceptance by God, and their own life after death, when each of those realities is supernatural? It may be trendy to minimize, downplay or ignore the bodily, physical, actual resurrection of Jesus Christ, but it is not wise because the gospel we hold out to the world is addressing actual, literal, physical concerns. Actual dying is a problem we cannot ignore. And surviving it without God's just condemnation is the crux of the gospel message. Because the problems being addressed by the gospel are tangible and real, God's attestation regarding his solution to our problem comes through tangible and real history.[3]

In a memorable scene, during Lazarus' funeral in Bethany just outside of Jerusalem, Jesus spoke directly to the ultimate issue when he said, *"I am the resurrection and the life. Whoever believes in me, though he die, yet shall he live, and everyone who lives and believes in me shall never die"* (Jn.11:25-

---

[3] For more on the historicity of Christ's resurrection consult Gary Habermas and Michael Licona's *The Case for the Resurrection of Jesus* (Kregel, 2004), Lee Strobel's *The Case for the Resurrection* (Zondervan, 2010), Gary Habermas' *The Risen Jesus and Future Hope* (Rowman & Littlefield, 2003), Josh McDowell's *The Resurrection Factor* (Here's Life, 1981), and Loranie Boettners' *Immortality* (P & R, 2004).

26). When Jesus speaks of death here, there are two aspects in view. There is biological death and the much more serious "second death", the reality of which Jesus warns about when he speaks of the relational separation and judgment of those "cast into outer darkness where there is weeping and gnashing of teeth" (Mt.22:13; 25:30; Lk.13:28; cp. Rev.2:11; 20:6; et al.). There are also two aspects in view when Jesus speaks of life. Not only is an incorruptible physical life granted to those who die trusting in Jesus (i.e., our future bodily resurrection – 1Cor.15:52-55; 1Th.4:14-18), but there is also an exemption from the eternal and irreversible "second death" (i.e., our future reception by God and his unencumbered blessings – Rev.2:11; 20:6). The real life Jesus came to secure for us, which was attested to by his resurrection, is the kind of life that is fully and eternally accepted by God and is lived in a newly reconstructed physical body which is impervious to decay, disease or any kind of death. This is the ultimate resolve and endgame for biblical Christianity:

> Then I saw a new heaven and a new earth,
> for the first heaven and the first earth had
> passed away, and the sea was no more. And I
> saw the holy city, new Jerusalem, coming
> down out of heaven from God, prepared as
> a bride adorned for her husband. And I heard
> a loud voice from the throne saying, "Behold,
> the dwelling place of God is with man. He will

dwell with them, and they will be his people, and God himself will be with them as their God. He will wipe away every tear from their eyes, and death shall be no more, neither shall there be mourning, nor crying, nor pain anymore, for the former things have passed away." And he who was seated on the throne said, "Behold, I am making all things new." Also he said, "Write this down, for these words are trustworthy and true." (Rev.21:1-5)

*Now when they heard this they were
cut to the heart, and said to Peter and
the rest of the apostles, "Brothers,
what shall we do?"*

Acts 2:37

Chapter 4
Repentance

These next two chapters are extremely important. We are going to dive in and look at a lot of biblical passages seeking to precisely understand what God's word teaches about what our response to the gospel message must be. Because of its pivotal importance, this part of the gospel has always been under attack and is often hotly debated. Since we cannot afford to misinterpret what God has said about these issues, the following discussion will require a certain level of detail. We will need to consider a variety of ancient words, trace the flow of biblical revelation, and attempt to comprehend what the response to the gospel means by paying close attention to biblical and theological contexts. So hang in there. If it feels too nitpicky or redundant, it's really not. It's just that we need to carefully shape our understanding of what God requires by looking at these commands from a number of angles. Ready? Here we go.

From Indicative to Imperative

The gospel is primarily a proclamation. As we have seen, it is a proclamation that Jesus has accomplished all that is required for sinful enemies of their Creator to be granted the status of forgiven sons and daughters of God. It is indisputable *good news* because what we were unable to fix as guilty and condemned transgressors, God out of his immense and costly love, has in Christ freely fixed for us. As a proclamation, a majority of the gospel is a message delivered in factual statements of completed action. When it comes to most of the gospel content: it has been done, it has been accomplished, it is finished!

However, the gospel is more than a proclamation, it is also a call. As one reads of the delivery of the gospel in the pages of Scripture it is hard to miss the verbal shift from the finished action of past tense verbs, to the urgency of present tense, imperative verbs. Once the facts of the gospel are proclaimed, the call of the gospel is conveyed with passion, persuasion and insistence. The move from proclamation to call is the consistent pattern we find throughout the New Testament beginning with Christ himself:

> Now after John was arrested, Jesus came into Galilee, proclaiming the gospel of God, and saying, "The time is fulfilled, and the kingdom of God is at hand; repent and believe in the gospel." (Mark 1:14-15)

The proclamation of what Christ has accomplished is a declaration of historical facts – they are true realities of things that have already happened. Responding to the imperative call of the gospel, on the other hand, is something that has actually happened for some, but not others. Many people have in fact responded to the gospel just as Christ commanded, but many more have not. And since the Bible is clear that in the end there are only two groups of people – those who are freed from the condemnation of their sins and those who bear the consequences of their sins – the crucial difference is one's response to the imperative call of the gospel. Nothing could be more important!

The Bible has a lot to say about the mystery of how this required response is divinely worked in the hearts and minds of people who are saved, but before we consider any of that it is critical that we carefully understand the meaning of the two oft repeated commands that follow the gospel indicatives. As we will see, to "repent" and "believe" (Mk.1:15) are two distinct yet inseparable components of one divinely worked response to the gospel proclamation, which takes place in the heart and mind of every person who becomes a Christian. It is the initiation of the Christian life, yet yields lasting, daily effects throughout the remainder of one's life on earth. Let's take a closer look at each component.

The Need for Repentance

Jesus tells a story of an unforgiven rich man who was sent to a "place of torment" after his death, Jesus said that the rich man grieved at the thought of his brothers coming to the same painful place when it came their turn to die. In Christ's story the rich man pleads with Abraham, who resides across *"a great chasm,"* for someone to be sent back from the dead to warn his brothers to avoid *"this place of torment."* Abraham responds by saying that his brothers have the Bible – *"Moses and the Prophets"*, and that they should be listening to them. The rich man objects and says, *"No father Abraham, but if someone goes to them from the dead, they will repent."* To which Abraham answers, *"If they do not hear Moses and the Prophets, neither will they be convinced if someone should rise from the dead"* (Lk.16:19-31).

Jesus memorably impresses upon us in this story that the difference between heaven and hell, from the pages of both the Old and New Testaments, is one's response to the biblical call to "repent!" The message of the saving work of Christ came into sharp focus in the New Testament era, but the call to repentance in order to be "saved" is nothing new.

If you go back through the Old Testament you will find an undeniable continuum as it relates to God's imperative call and the riches of his forgiveness. See this in Solomon's prayer, as he affirms the relationship between repentance and forgiveness.

> *...if they turn their heart in the land to which they have been carried captive, and repent and plead with you in the land of their captors, saying, 'We have sinned and have acted perversely and wickedly,' if they repent with all their mind and with all their heart in*

> *the land of their enemies, who carried them*
> *captive, and pray to you toward their land,*
> *which you gave to their fathers, the city that*
> *you have chosen, and the house that I have*
> *built for your name, then hear in heaven*
> *your dwelling place their prayer and their*
> *plea, and maintain their cause and forgive*
> *your people who have sinned against you,*
> *and all their transgressions that they have*
> *committed against you, and grant them*
> *compassion in the sight of those who carried*
> *them captive, that they may have compassion*
> *on them.* *(1 Kings 8:47-50)*

David warns that the unrepentant will not be forgiven, but instead bear the divine consequences of their sins:

> *God is a righteous judge, and a God who feels*
> *indignation every day. If a man does not*
> *repent, God will whet his sword; he has*
> *bent and readied his bow; he has prepared*
> *for him his deadly weapons, making his*
> *arrows fiery shafts. (Psalm 7:11-13)*

Isaiah speaks of God's righteous work of redemption and its relation to the repentant heart when he writes, *"Zion shall be redeemed by justice, and those in her who repent, by righteousness"* (Is.1:27).

Jesus certainly affirmed this connection in his preaching. When some in the crowd were pondering the divine motives behind two calamities, which had recently taken place in their society, Jesus turns their attention to their own lives and their need for repentance.

> *There were some present at that very time who told him about the Galileans whose blood Pilate had mingled with their sacrifices. And he answered them, "Do you think that these Galileans were worse sinners than all the other Galileans, because they suffered in this way? No, I tell you; but unless you repent, you will all likewise perish. Or those eighteen on whom the tower in Siloam fell and killed them: do you think that they were worse offenders than all the others who lived in Jerusalem? No, I tell you; but unless you repent, you will all likewise perish."*
> *(Lk 13:1-5)*

Jesus affirms the universality of sin and with urgency calls the crowd to repent so that they will enjoy God's grace instead of his just retribution. Of course Christ's life, death and resurrection provide the means of forgiveness. But even after the completion of his redemptive work on earth, he commissions his followers to take the message of repentance and forgiveness to the entire world.

Then he said to them, "These are my words that I spoke to you while I was still with you, that everything written about me in the Law of Moses and the Prophets and the Psalms must be fulfilled." Then he opened their minds to understand the Scriptures, and said to them, "Thus it is written, that the Christ should suffer and on the third day rise from the dead, and that repentance and forgiveness of sins should be proclaimed in his name to all nations, beginning from Jerusalem." (Lk.24:44-47)

And this is precisely what we see throughout the history of the early church as recorded in the New Testament. Note this record of the apostolic message.

Repent, therefore, and turn again, that your sins may be blotted out. (Acts 3:19)

And they glorified God, saying, "Then to the Gentiles also God has granted repentance that leads to life." (Acts 11:18)

The times of ignorance God overlooked, but now he commands all people everywhere to repent, because he has fixed a day on which he will judge the world in righteousness by a man whom he has appointed; and of this he

> *has given assurance to all by raising him*
> *from the dead. (Acts 17:30-31)*

> *For godly grief produces a repentance that*
> *leads to salvation without regret, whereas*
> *worldly grief produces death.*
> *(2 Corinthians 7:10)*

> *The Lord is not slow to fulfill his promise, as*
> *some count slowness, but is patient toward*
> *you, not wishing that any should perish, but*
> *that all should reach repentance.*
> *(2 Peter 3:9)*

Repentance is obviously an indispensible component of God's required response to the gospel, but what precisely does it mean? How does one repent? What does it look like? Is it an emotional reaction? Is it a cerebral decision? How will I know if I have repented? To answer these questions, let's take a closer look at the word, its usage and, examples of it in the Bible.

The "Turning" of *Shub*

The Old Testament word that God chose to express the required response to his promise of forgiveness is the Hebrew word *shub*. The word *shub* is used 1,054 times in the Hebrew Scriptures, It carries a directional sense to it, or more precisely, a "re-directional" sense. Besides the English word "repent," *shub* is translated in the English Standard Version into words like "turn," "return," "recede" and "go back." The word *shub* is sometimes used side-by-side in differing grammatical forms to help describe the "turning" of repentance.

> *Therefore say to the house of Israel, Thus says the Lord GOD: Repent [shub] and turn away [shub] from your idols, and turn away your faces from all your abominations. (Ezekiel 14:6)[1]*

Sometimes the directional sense of the word *shub* is accentuated by its use in combination with other conceptually related words such as *azub*, which carries the idea of "leaving," "abandoning," "deserting" or "rejecting" the things from which one is repenting. Notice the combination here:

> *Seek the LORD while he may be found; call upon him while he is near; let the wicked forsake [azub] his way, and the unrighteous man his thoughts; let him return [shub] to the LORD, that he may have compassion on him, and to our God, for he will abundantly pardon. (Isaiah 55:6-7)*

Repentance clearly carries the re-directional

---

[1] See also Ezekiel 18:30 where the same pattern of *shub* in the Qal and Hiphil are combined for emphasis and explanation.

idea of turning around. Turning around necessarily involves leaving something behind in order to go the other way. When we see the word repentance utilized in reference to God's forgiveness, the object being left behind is sin. People are called to turn from their participation, connection and involvement in sinful attitudes, words and behaviors. To illustrate, consider the use of these same words in a practical setting in the Book of Ruth. After Ruth the Moabite and her Jewish mother-in-law Naomi are both widowed, Naomi decides to leave Moab to live again in Israel. As Naomi begins the journey home she encourages Ruth to "turn around" (*shub*) and go back to her own country of Moab, which would necessarily involve "leaving behind" (*azub*) her mother-in-law. Ruth says to Naomi:

> "Do not urge me to leave [azub] you or to
> return [shub] from following you."
> (Ruth 1:16)

Sometimes the words we find in conjunction with *shub* vividly depict the notion of "leaving behind" what is being "repented of." Words like *shalak* express the decisive repulsion associated with one's turn from sin. Shalak contains the graphic picture of "dropping," "tossing," "expelling" or "throwing" something away.

> Repent [shub] and turn from [shub] all your
> transgressions, lest iniquity be your ruin.

70

> *Cast away from you [shalak] all the*
> *transgressions that you have committed*
> *(Ezekiel 18:30-31)*

God's communication of the idea of repentance in the Old Testament gives us clarity about what God expects. He is calling sinful people to turn away from sinful thoughts and actions, leaving behind their involvement in what is unrighteous. As we will later see, this does not imply that we are enabled to live perfectly, but repentance will clearly result in a changed life.

The "Turning" of Metanoia

In the New Testament the words that translate "repent" are *metanoia* (the noun) and *metanoeo* (the verb). These words occur a total of fifty-six times in the New Testament and are usually found in passages where the gospel is being preached. This term in the New Testament, as well as in the Old, serves to depict the response of those whom God forgives. Notice the centrality of "repentance" in Christ's commission to take his message to the nations:

> *Then [Jesus] opened their minds to*
> *understand the Scriptures, and said to them,*
> *"Thus it is written, that the Christ should*
> *suffer and on the third day rise from the*
> *dead, and that repentance and forgiveness of*
> *sins should be proclaimed in his name to all*

nations, beginning from Jerusalem.'
(Luke 24:45-47)

In the Book of Acts the term is portrayed as the difference between those who acquire God's gift of life and those who don't.

> "If then God gave the same gift to them as he gave to us when we believed in the Lord Jesus Christ, who was I that I could stand in God's way?" When they heard these things they fell silent. And they glorified God, saying, "Then to the Gentiles also God has granted repentance that leads to life."
> (Acts 11:17-18)

The word *metanoia*, as with its Hebrew predecessor *shub*, carries the idea of "turning" from sin to God. You can find that in some English Bibles *metanoia* is translated "turn back", "turn away" and "turn from."[2] *Metanoia* clearly depicts the reorientation of the direction of one's life. Paul describes this reorientation in his evangelistic preaching when he calls people to repentance, articulating clearly the Person to whom they are to turn.

---

[2] As in Tyndale House Publisher's 1996 *New Living Translation* in Revelation 2:5; 2:21 and 3:19 respectively. Often these translators provide the words "turn" and "repent" when translating the word *metanoia*. This occurs in the NLT eighteen times throughout the Gospels and the Book of Acts.

> I *did not shrink from declaring to you*
> *anything that was profitable, and teaching*
> *you in public and from house to house,*
> *testifying both to Jews and to Greeks of*
> *repentance toward God and of faith in our*
> *Lord Jesus Christ. (Acts 20:20–21)*

Elsewhere, in the record of evangelistic preaching in Acts, we read of what people are directed to turn from.

> *...we bring you good news, that you should*
> *turn from these vain things to a living God,*
> *who made the heaven and the earth and the*
> *sea and all that is in them. (Acts 14:15b)*

Here, the word translated "turn" which carries the idea of repentance is *epistrepho*. We find this word elucidating and enforcing the sense of *metanoia* in Peter's preaching:

> *Repent [metanoia] therefore, and turn again*
> *[epistrepho], that your sins may be blotted*
> *out (Acts 3:19)*

Paul also uses both of these words when describing his own calling and preaching:

> *The Lord said, "...I am sending you to open*
> *their eyes, so that they may turn [epistrepho]*

> from darkness to light and from the power
> of Satan to God, that they may receive
> forgiveness of sins..." Therefore, O King
> Agrippa, I was not disobedient to the
> heavenly vision, but declared first to those in
> Damascus, then in Jerusalem and throughout
> all the region of Judea, and also to the
> Gentiles, that they should repent [metanoia]
> and turn [epistrepho] to God, performing
> deeds in keeping with their repentance."
> (Acts 26:15–20)

The call of the "about-face" of repentance is also
seen in John the Baptist's preaching in the continued
interchange of the words *metanoia* and *epistrepho*.
John's preaching was characterized by a call to
"repentance" (*metanoia*) and was summarized before
his birth as a ministry of turning (*epistrepho*) people
to God.

> In those days John the Baptist came
> preaching in the wilderness of Judea, "Repent
> [metanoia], for the kingdom of heaven is at
> hand." (Matthew 3:1-2)

> And he will turn [epistrepho] many of
> the children of Israel to the Lord their God
> (Luke 1:16)

The first component of the required response of

the gospel is repentance. It is a call to turn from sin to God. It is a call to turn away from a life of sinful actions, sinful thoughts and sinful independence from God. It begins in the mind and always finds its way into one's life. Some have tried to limit the characterization of repentance to a mere mental activity, which may or may not be evidenced in one's life. This is clearly something less than what is described in the Bible.

Repentance – More than Changed Thoughts

Couched in a concern to keep the gospel free from adding a requirement of works, some have strongly sought to redefine and recast repentance as a synonym of faith, or as a simple change of mind about who Christ is. As such, modern Bible teachers have often campaigned that the idea of turning from sin to God is superfluous and injurious to the biblical gospel.[3]

Advocates of this kind of reductionism have pointed to the etymology of the word "repentance."

---

[3] Tragically, this is why many can testify to having attended church for years without ever hearing of the concept or the word "repentance." Some modern preachers will excuse their omission by citing its absence in Acts 16:31 where it states that Paul responded to the Philippian jailer's question of how to be saved by telling him to "believe" [*pisteo*]. Of course this summary of Paul's answer also did not include any information about God, sin, the cross, or the resurrection of Christ. Which of course are all essential to the gospel. Such logic also does not take into account the next verse in Acts 16 which tells us that Paul continued and "spoke the word of the Lord to him" (v.32).

Metanoia, they point out, is made up of two Greek words, *meta* which means "with" or "after," and *noia* which means "to perceive," "to understand" or "to think." So *meta-noia* they argue, simply means to "think-after" or to "perceive [differently] after" as in changing one's mind or opinion of something. Changing one's mind *about Christ* is the meaning they claim is intended throughout the New Testament when the word *Metanoia* is associated with the gospel.

This etymological approach has been convincing for many, but it cannot stand up to scrutiny when we allow the biblical usage to define the word. Clearly this is not what is in view when repentance is presented to us in Scripture. Turning from sin to God is obviously what is intended in the numerous passages already cited. The combination of *metanoia* with *epistrepho* gives us an undeniable picture of what God is commanding. The choice of the word *metanoia* for the Hebrew word *shub* in the Septuagint (i.e., the pre-Christian Greek translation of the Hebrew Old Testament) should rule out any attempts to water down this important biblical word. [4]

Remember that our English dictionaries define English words by our contextual usage and not their component etymology. You would not allow someone to define your use of the words "awful," "passage" or

---

[4] See Craig Bloomberg's discussion of *shub* and *metanoia* in *A Handbook of New Testament Exegesis*, Baker Academic, 2010, p. 133.

"hamlet" based on their research of the words "awe," "full," "pass," "age," "ham" and "let." Likewise, we have to form our understanding of biblical words from their use in biblical contexts.[5]

With that said, it is certainly conceded that repentance involves one's mind. It begins with an internal, thoughtful turning from sin. A purposeful, intentional turning from any behavior presupposes a mental redirection. If you purpose to stop biting your fingernails or eating cheeseburgers, such a "turning" starts in your mind. But the reality of your "turning" is evidenced by your future behavior – whether you are still biting your fingernails or eating cheeseburgers. When it comes to the sinful life from which we are commanded to repent, it is admittedly a change that involves my mind, but it is clearly not biblical repentance (or a turning away) unless my future actions demonstrate that change. This is why the following directives are associated with the call to biblical repentance:

> *Bear fruit in keeping with repentance.*
> *(Matthew 3:8)*

> *repent and turn to God, performing deeds in keeping with their repentance. (Acts 26:20b)*

> *For godly grief produces a repentance that*

---

[5] See the chapter entitled "Word Study Fallacies" in D.A. Carson's *Exegetical Fallacies, Second Edition,* Baker Academic, 1996.

> *leads to salvation without regret, whereas*
> *worldly grief produces death. For see what*
> *earnestness this godly grief has produced*
> *in you, but also what eagerness to clear*
> *yourselves, what indignation, what fear, what*
> *longing, what zeal, (2 Corinthians 7:10–11a)*

Repentance is the commanded response to the gospel proclamation regarding the finished work of Christ. It is a call to turn from sin to God. But having clarity about what repentance means may still leave us looking for a further explanation of what repentance looks like in our lives here and now.

Turning from Sin to God

Sin, as we discussed in chapter two, is a reality for each of us from moment of conception (Ps.51:5). We are born as sinners, alienated and relationally separated from God. Our sinful state can be summarized as a life of detachment from God, or perhaps more personally, as an inborn directional orientation to please ourselves, not God. We are all born living for ourselves, for our own satisfaction, forming and following our own agendas. We are *"like sheep without a shepherd"* (Mt.9:36), not *"seeking after God"* (Rom.3:11), *"turned, everyone, to his own way"* (Is.53:6). Repentance at the most fundamental level is a turning from a life of self-direction and self-management to living a life for God and his agenda.

Paul underscores this central aspect of repentance when he writes,

> ...[Christ] died for all, that those who live
> might no longer live for themselves but
> for him who for their sake died and was
> raised. *(2 Corinthians 5:15)*

Repentance is a turning from a life of independent, self-determined decision-making. It is a mindset that recognizes that Christ-followers are *"to live for the rest of the time in the flesh no longer for human passions but for the will of God"* (1Pt.4:2). In response to the grace and mercy of God to save us, we are called to see our lives as his.

> *I appeal to you therefore, brothers, by the
> mercies of God, to present your bodies as a
> living sacrifice, holy and acceptable to God,
> which is your rational service.*[6] *Do not be
> conformed to this world, but be transformed
> by the renewal of your mind, that by testing
> you may discern what is the will of God, what*

---

[6] "Rational service" is the ESV's marginal translation of *logiken latreian* found in the footnote, which arguably fits the context much more consistently than what most think of with the words "spiritual worship." For the complexity of these words see Douglas J. Moo *The Epistle to the Romans*, The New International Commentary on the New Testament, Eerdmans Publishing, 1996, pp. 751-754.

is good and acceptable and perfect.
(Romans 12:1-2)

The grace of God which saves us, now instructs us to consider our lives as his – repenting or turning from a life lived for ourselves and instead living for God. The response to the gospel is a turning to no longer thinking of my life as my own.

This is the reason so much of our identity in the New Testament is summed up in the word *doulos,* which means "slave." As non-Christians we are described as being "enslaved" to our own agendas, desires and direction – which is the definition of sin. Christ "frees" us from sin and "enslaves" us to God and his righteous agenda.

> *But thanks be to God, that you who were once slaves of sin have become obedient from the heart to the standard of teaching to which you were committed, and, having been set free from sin, have become slaves of righteousness. I am speaking in human terms, because of your natural limitations. For just as you once presented your members as slaves to impurity and to lawlessness leading to more lawlessness, so now present your members as slaves to righteousness leading to sanctification. For when you were slaves of sin, you were free in regard to righteousness. But what fruit were you*

> *getting at that time from the things of which*
> *you are now ashamed? For the end of those*
> *things is death. But now that you have been*
> *set free from sin and have become slaves of*
> *God, the fruit you get leads to sanctification*
> *and its end, eternal life. (Romans 6:17–22)*

This radical redirection of your life, to live no longer for yourself, but for God and his righteous agenda is your new identity. This is powerfully illustrated throughout the New Testament by the image of "slaves of God"– lives owned and directed by our Creator.[7] The gospel calls for this reorientation, this initial and continual repentance from the independent and self-serving direction of our lives.

Such a forthright description of repentance may give some insight into why repentance is often downplayed, redefined or ignored in many popular presentations of what all too often passes for the gospel. Biblical calls to this kind of radical reorientation would make "self-denial" and the "lordship" of Christ foundational and not optional. Which is exactly what we find when we read the New Testament.

> *And calling the crowd to him with his*
> *disciples, [Jesus] said to them, "If anyone*
> *would come after me, let him deny himself*

---

[7] See John MacArthur's extended treatment of the imagery, use, and implications of doulos in his book *Slave: The Hidden Truth of Your Identity in Christ,* Thomas Nelson Publishers, 2010.

and take up his cross and follow me. For whoever would save his life will lose it, but whoever loses his life for my sake and the gospel's will save it. For what does it profit a man to gain the whole world and forfeit his soul? For what can a man give in return for his soul?" (Mark 8:34–37)

Becoming a Christian begins with an understanding that we are giving up the controls of our lives. The old bumper sticker that reads, "God is my co-pilot," is a theological impossibility. God doesn't agree to assume such a position in anyone's life. Christ calls us to give up the driver's seat. Again, this is clearly seen in the self-denial of repentance throughout the teaching of Christ. Jesus said, *"So therefore, any one of you who does not renounce all that he has cannot be my disciple"* (Luke 14:33).

The word "renounce" (*apotasso*) is part and parcel of the concept of repentance. If I am turning from the independence of living for myself to living for God, then I am "leaving behind" or "renouncing" the oversight, management and lordship of everything I have.

This has lead some of the confused and frustrated to retort, "So what am I supposed to do to become a Christian, sign over my bank accounts to the church, leave my job and sign up to be a missionary?" While there were a handful of such immediate and dramatic occurrences during the earthly ministry and evangelism of Christ (e.g., Mt.19:16-30 and Mk.1:16-20), the call of repentance begins with a willingness. In time, God's specific direction makes itself clear as he guides penitent people through an increased understanding of his word and the undeniable conviction of his Spirit. In the Bible we often see a call to repentance where people are sent right back to their homes and their old jobs, in order to live new lives for God in their former contexts (e.g., Lk.8:38-39; Lk.3:10-14).

Jesus provides an illustration of what repentance looks like that is quite helpful. He said,

> *"Or what king, going out to encounter another king in war, will not sit down first and deliberate whether he is able with ten thousand to meet him who comes against him with twenty thousand? And if not, while the other is yet a great way off, he sends a delegation and asks for terms of peace. So therefore, any one of you who does not renounce all that he has cannot be my disciple." (Luke 14:31–33)*

When an outgunned king in a battle *"asks for terms of peace,"* it is never an agreement to go our separate ways. The superior and stronger king "takes control" of the inferior and weaker king's property. That calls off the war, but it radically changes the arrangement for the losing king. These "terms of peace" are also known as surrender. One king surrenders to another king and therefore turns over or "renounces" all that he has. The old king and his kingdom are now under new management. There is a new "Lord" overseeing everything. Now consider yourself as a part of the conquered kingdom. The new "Lord" may keep you doing the same thing you were doing before, but now you are doing it for him. Or the new "Lord" may want to move you into a new role, a new occupation, or a new part of the kingdom. The bottom line is you must realize that the conquering king is now in charge and you are subject to his leadership.

All this talk of a repentance that results in "slavery," "lordship" and "subjection" may lead to an image of hostility between you and God. But of course the complete opposite is true. Before our repentance we were at odds with God, we were in fact his enemies (Rom.5:10). But as repentant Christians, a loving Father now rules us. He is in charge and we are in subjection to him. But he is a benevolent dictator. He loves us and wants what is best, not only for his glory, but also for our good. When we surrender in repentance to him, he will lead us in a way that is ultimately best. It may not be easy, and it may not always feel good, but in the end we will see that it was all for an ultimate good. God is for us and our repentance is the beginning of realizing his transcendent goodness.

*And we know that for those who love God
all things work together for good, for
those who are called according to his
purpose. For those whom he foreknew he
also predestined to be conformed to the
image of his Son, in order that he might be
the firstborn among many brothers. And
those whom he predestined he also called,
and those whom he called he also justified,
and those whom he justified he also glorified.
What then shall we say to these things? If
God is for us, who can be against us?
(Romans 8:28–31)*

And without faith it is impossible to please him...

Hebrews 11:6

Chapter 5
Faith

"Faith" is one of the most common words associated with Christianity – as well as every other religion for that matter. Sometimes you find the word used to describe the whole spectrum of religions as when someone asks, "What faith are you?" Sometimes you find it employed to summarize the Christian life in general, with statements like, "I kept the faith." Other times it is used as a central Christian virtue, as when people say, "You need more faith."

But what does the word mean, especially as it relates to getting it right with God? How does the Bible use the term? And how is it often misunderstood?

The Biblical Definition of "Faith"

The story is told of a group of second grade Sunday School kids whose teacher asked, "What is faith?" One child enthusiastically raised his hand and blurted out, "Faith is believing something you know isn't true."

Unfortunately, that's not far from the definition many misguided grown-ups would give if pressed. But it is certainly not what the Bible means by faith. Faith is presented to us in Scripture as a confidence in what is true. The Old Testament Hebrew word group translated "faith" is also translated "truth," "truly" and "certain."[1] The New Testament Greek word translated "faith" likewise carries the idea of something or someone in whom confidence can be placed, as is evidenced by English words such as "faithfulness," "reliability," "fidelity" and "commitment."[2]

Of course the Bible affirms not only what is readily seen or already experienced, but also what God promises he will do in the future. This is a big part of where the idea that faith means confidence in what is "unseen" comes from. God has given us a whole set of promises that he will make things right in the future – he will eradicate evil, he will execute justice, he will count us righteous in Christ, he will usher in a new world free from imperfection. Based on God's prophetic track record and the manifestation of his power and fidelity displayed in Christ's first coming, Christians have firm confidence that God will do what he says concerning the future.

Even before we encounter the word "faith" in the Bible, we see God telling his creation that he will fix what's wrong and correct the problems. "Trust me" is implicit in a long series of promises - from the guarantees to "bruise the serpent's head" and "blessing the world through Abraham's offspring," all

---

[1] See the word group *AMN* (#116) in Laird, Harris, Archer and Waltke's *Theological Wordbook of the Old Testament* (Moody Press, 1999), vol. 1, pp. 51-53.

[2] See the words *pistis* and *pistos* in Arndt, Danker and Bauer's *A Greek-English Lexicon of the New Testament and Other Early Christian Literature.* 3rd ed. (University of Chicago Press, 2000), pp. 818-821.

the way to creating "a new heavens and a new earth" (Gen.3:15; Gen.12:3; Is.65:17).

As it relates to the future, this is how faith is depicted in the Bible. Hebrews 11:1 tells us, *"faith is the assurance of things hoped for, the conviction of things not seen."* This is not a wishful, cross-your-fingers kind of faith, but an assurance based on what God has said and what he has already done and that God will continue to do exactly what he has said he will do.

How "Faith" Relates to the Gospel

More specifically, "faith" is associated with the gospel. Faith is the second distinguishable component of our required response to the good news. We are called to turn from sin to God and trust in his provision for our salvation.

Like the word "repentance," the word "faith" is often associated with the forgiveness of sins.

> *And when Jesus saw their faith, he said to the paralytic, "Son, your sins are forgiven." (Mark 2:5)*

> *And he said to her, "Your sins are forgiven." Then those who were at table with him began to say among themselves, "Who is this, who even forgives sins?" And he said to the woman, "Your faith has saved you; go in*

peace." (Luke 7:48–50)

*...having cleansed their hearts by faith.
(Acts 15:9b)*

*"so that they may turn from darkness to light
and from the power of Satan to God, that
they may receive forgiveness of sins and a
place among those who are sanctified by
faith in me." (Acts 26:18)*

*For we hold that one is justified by faith apart
from works of the law. (Romans 3:28)*

Together, faith and repentance are seen as the starting point of the Christian life; together these terms represent the response that God requires from those who receive forgiveness of sins. This is why we see these important words paired together in biblical contexts that relate to evangelism. For instance, Paul summarizes his outreach efforts in the city of Ephesus as *"testifying both to Jews and to Greeks of repentance toward God and of faith in our Lord Jesus Christ"* (Ac.20:21). The writer of Hebrews refers to both of these required components of the gospel response, that is, *"repentance from dead works and faith toward God,"* as the *"elementary doctrine of Christ"* (Heb.6:1).

Faith, Belief & *Pistis*

It is hard to overestimate the importance of this next observation as it relates to the biblical call to respond to the gospel. The word "believe" is translated from the same Greek word that translates "faith." The noun in the Greek New Testament is *pistis* and the verb is *pisteuo*. They both translate "faith," "belief" and "believe." The identical phrase that translates "repentance and faith" is elsewhere translated "repent and believe." This would not be such a big deal if the words "faith" and "believe" carried synonymous meanings, but in the minds of most English speakers they do not.

Note the usage of the word *pisteuo* in the following passages.

> *Now after John was arrested, Jesus came into Galilee, proclaiming the gospel of God, and saying, "The time is fulfilled, and the kingdom of God is at hand; repent and believe [pisteuo] in the gospel." (Mark 1:14–15)*

> *And Paul said, "John baptized with the baptism of repentance, telling the people to believe [pisteuo] in the one who was to come after him, that is, Jesus." (Acts 19:4)*

> *And the hand of the Lord was with them, and a great number who believed [pisteuo]*

turned to the Lord. (Acts 11:21)

It is unfortunate that the word "believe" is so often understood as mentally agreeing with some facts. But that is not what the words *pistis* and *pisteuo* mean. These words speak of a confident trust and not a mental assent. Scholars of all stripes and varieties, who are familiar with the Greek language of the New Testament, can attest to the frustration of this common misunderstanding.

> *The key terms repent and believe have remained unchanged from the first great English translations of Tyndale in 1526... In the meantime, these English terms have taken on specific meanings of their own, which have moved them farther and farther away from the underlying Greek. Believe is now used mostly in the mental sense, 'accept as true,' and only secondarily is it 'have confidence in, trust.' The second, and not the first, sense is the primary meaning of the Greek verb pisteuo and other related words, such as the noun pistis, usually translated 'faith.' But the common understanding of believe has overpowered the basic sense of faith, so that both have come to signify mental activity: accept a statement as true. As a result, in traditional English versions Jesus' message comes out, 'Accept the words*

> *I say as true,' when Jesus is actually calling
> on his hearers to put their trust in the good
> news. And when the distraught father tells
> Jesus, in traditional language, 'I believe, help
> my unbelief' (Mk.9:24), it sounds like he
> is trying to convince himself to 'accept as
> true' something that is not. Actually, he is
> exclaiming, 'I do trust! Help my lack of
> trust!'"*[3]

It is critically important that we never allow the power of the words *pistis* and *pisteuo* to be understood as simply acknowledging a set of facts. And yet this is precisely what some people think is required of those who would have their sins forgiven.

Some people, when asked whether they are Christians answer, "I believe in God." By which they mean, "I accept the fact that there is a God." or "I affirm that the God of the Bible is real." Since the word "believe" is presented in the Bible as the required response to the gospel, they assume that because they uphold a belief that God indeed exists, they are forgiven Christians. Some go further and say they "believe in Jesus" which means, "I believe in the historical Jesus of the Bible."

Often when people are told that they are supposed to believe in the gospel, they are quick to agree that they affirm the facts of the gospel message

[3] Daryl Schmidt, *The Gospel of Mark – The Scholars Bible* (Polebridge Press, 1991) pp. 24-25.

– that is, they agree people are sinful, and that Jesus died on the cross and rose from the dead. It is also not uncommon to hear preachers add that what a person really needs to do is not only believe the facts, but believe that those facts are true for them. In other words, the requirement is not just believing that Jesus died, it's believing that Christ died for you. I've heard these definitions of faith countless times. Tragically, that is not what *pistis* means. Faith is not simply affirming a set of facts, even if one includes himself as the beneficiary of those facts.

Faith as a Transfer of Trust

Pistis is presented to us in the Bible as a transferring of trust. God requires that those who would be forgiven, direct their confidence toward him and his provision for our need. The Bible clearly calls us to place our assurance and confidence in what God has done for us.

This transference of trust is clearly seen in the addition of prepositions that often follow the word *pistis*. If a mere affirmation of facts was intended by the word pistis, we would not expect words such as "in," "on" and "upon" to follow.[4] To believe in or on something or someone communicates more than a mere mental assent to a set of facts.

---

[4] The words which are often found in combination with *pistis* are the Greek preposition: *en* (on or in), *eis* (in or into) *epi* (on or upon). English versions will variously translate these phrases "believe in" or "believe on."

For instance, notice the difference in the questions, "Do you believe me?" or "Do you believe in me?" If I told you what I had for lunch yesterday and then asked, "Do you believe me?" you would naturally consider the question to be a request to affirm some facts. If, on the other hand, you were to walk into my office and I asked, "Do you believe in me?" the question would carry an entirely different weight. The addition of these prepositions is quite important in helping us to understand what the required response to the gospel actually is.

Note how the word "in" follows the word "believe."[5]

> *"Do you believe in the Son of Man?" He answered, "And who is he, sir, that I may believe in him?" " (John 9:35b–36)*

> *Jesus answered them, "This is the work of God, that you believe in him whom he has sent." (John 6:29)*

> *Though he had done so many signs before them, they still did not believe in him (John 12:37)*

> *For it has been granted to you that for the sake of Christ you should not only believe in*

---

[5] The ESV translators translated all three combinations (i.e., *pistis en, pistis eis* and *pistis epi*) as "believe in."

him but also suffer for his sake
(Philippians 1:29)

I write these things to you who believe in the
name of the Son of God that you may know
that you have eternal life. (1 John 5:13)

To believe in Christ, or trust in Christ, leads us to ask the question, "Trust in him for what?" Of course the context of this repeated phrase is that we are to trust in him for our salvation – the forgiveness of our sins and our acceptance before God. We are required to trust in Christ to do for us what we are unable to do for ourselves. Before I expand on that, it may be helpful to point out two other contexts in which the above phrase is used in the New Testament. The first is found in a summary of Christ's initial preaching. Mark writes, *"Now after John was arrested, Jesus came into Galilee, proclaiming the gospel of God, and saying, 'The time is fulfilled, and the kingdom of God is at hand; repent and believe in the gospel'"* (Mark 1:14–15). Here Christ says, "believe in the gospel." He is asking us to believe the good news that we can be made right with God. Of course that is simply a broader way of saying "believe in Christ." For the gospel calls us to do just that.

Elsewhere we find statements like this one from John 14:1, *"Let not your hearts be troubled. Believe in God; believe also in me"* (John 14:1). Here Jesus says to not only believe in Christ (and not only the gospel) but also in God. Of course there should be no confusion here. To believe in God to be saved, is to believe in the message of salvation, which is to believe in the Person who accomplished salvation for us.

The difference between mental assent concerning some facts and a trust in someone is aptly illustrated by the following story of a daredevil who entertains the crowds by walking a tightrope strung across Niagara Falls. He nimbly walks back and forth, accompanied by the approving cheers of the crowd. Then, to up the ante, he walks a wheelbarrow full of bricks across the tightrope. The audience erupts in applause. The entertainer then asks the crowd, "How many of you believe I can put a person in this wheelbarrow and walk him across?" The admiring crowd affirms their belief that he can do it. Then he asks, "Who of you will get in the wheelbarrow?" There is a radical difference between believing someone and believing in someone!

God is not asking us to simply believe Christ or his message. God is requiring that we trust in Christ to take us across the threshold of this life and move us safely into the next. And that by trusting in Jesus, we will arrive there as accepted, forgiven and approved people, completely adequate to stand before our Creator and Judge.

Trusting in Christ, Not Ourselves

The major focus of the gospel is a transfer of trust

from ourselves to Christ. When God says he will take care of our problem, we are called to be confident that he will – that he has. We are called to no longer trust in anything else. When it comes to getting it right before God, our tendency is to think that we can do it ourselves, or that we can do it with a little help from God.

Ask the average person if he will be okay on Judgment Day and enter heaven, he will likely say, "I hope so" or "I'm trying." Many default to the "scales theory" we talked about in chapter 2. They are trying and hoping that their good efforts will win the day. They think that perhaps the supposed "good deeds" they have done will be enough to outweigh their "bad deeds." In this all-too-common scenario the person is clearly trusting in themselves and the good they perceive they have done.

Others with some religious affiliation will say, "I am trying and with Jesus' help I will make it." They view their salvation as a team effort. Often they trust in their religious rituals or ceremonies along with Christ's supplementary assistance. Again, this team-effort approach still includes a good bit of trust in themselves. Neither of these approaches will do.

The biblical gospel calls us to trust that Jesus did it *all* for us and that our efforts account for nothing. Note carefully how Paul describes the gospel to the Philippians.

*For we... glory in Christ Jesus and put no
confidence in the flesh— though I myself
have reason for confidence in the flesh also.
If anyone else thinks he has reason for
confidence in the flesh, I have more:
circumcised on the eighth day, of the people
of Israel, of the tribe of Benjamin, a Hebrew
of Hebrews; as to the law, a Pharisee; as to
zeal, a persecutor of the church; as to
righteousness under the law, blameless. But
whatever gain I had, I counted as loss for
the sake of Christ. Indeed, I count everything
as loss because of the surpassing worth
of knowing Christ Jesus my Lord. For his
sake I have suffered the loss of all things and
count them as rubbish, in order that I may
gain Christ and be found in him, not having
a righteousness of my own that comes from
the law, but that which comes through faith
in Christ, the righteousness from God that
depends on faith (Philippians 3:3–9)*

Paul examines the theoretical "righteousness" of
his own resumé and says that even though it may
outshine the next guy's, the gospel has required him
to transfer his trust from any of those "righteous"
things, to the righteousness provided by Christ's
life. He considers any value of his "good deeds" as
nothing before God and has placed all of his trust
in the goodness or righteousness of Christ. This, he

says, is what makes him acceptable before God.

It comes down to the person we are trusting in. We all face this choice. We need to trust in Christ alone to make us acceptable before God. We cannot trust in ourselves or some hybrid of our works and what Christ has accomplished. What we need to do is exchange our resumé for Christ's. We are being called to place our complete confidence in Jesus alone.

This is where so many religious people get tripped up. They think that because they are comparatively "better" than the next guy, then it makes sense that God will take some of their good works into account to save them. But that is not what the Bible tells us.

Recall the parable Jesus told about the Pharisee and the tax collector. Notice Christ is driving home the point that our "justification" before a holy God is all about where our trust is.

> He also told this parable to some who trusted
> in themselves that they were righteous, and
> treated others with contempt: "Two men
> went up into the temple to pray, one a
> Pharisee and the other a tax collector. The
> Pharisee, standing by himself, prayed thus:
> 'God, I thank you that I am not like other
> men, extortioners, unjust, adulterers, or even
> like this tax collector. I fast twice a week; I
> give tithes of all that I get.' But the tax
> collector, standing far off, would not even lift
> up his eyes to heaven, but beat his breast,

> saying, 'God, be merciful to me, a sinner!' I
> tell you, this man went down to his house
> justified, rather than the other."
> (Luke 18:9–14a)

We either trust in ourselves or we trust in God's merciful provision. Trusting in ourselves, our religious activities or our charitable deeds will lead us to miss the grace of God. However, this grace is found by anyone – Pharisee or tax collector – who is obedient to the call of the gospel to transfer his trust from himself to God's gracious provision in the person and work of Christ.

Never Confuse the Role of Good Works

Of course the Bible continually calls Christians to do good. Jesus said, *"You are the light of the world... let your light shine before others, so that they may see your good works and give glory to your Father in heaven"* (Mt.5:14-16). When we do good, God is pleased and other people are pointed to him. But we dare not think that our good works add to or in any way contribute to our acceptance before God. Over and over again this point is made in the Bible.

> we know that a person is not justified by
> works of the law but through faith in Jesus
> Christ, so we also have believed in Christ
> Jesus, in order to be justified by faith in

> *Christ and not by works of the law, because by works of the law no one will be justified. (Galatians 2:16)*

If our good behavior made us right before God, we would be working to earn a divine paycheck. But Scripture goes to great lengths to tell us that this is not the case.

> *Now to the one who works, his wages are not counted as a gift but as his due. And to the one who does not work but believes in him who justifies the ungodly, his faith is counted as righteousness... (Romans 4:4–5)*

Even the best among us cannot contribute to their salvation. Our acceptance is earned for us, completely, through the perfectly righteous life of Christ.

> *For by works of the law no human being will be justified in his sight (Romans 3:20)*

> *Then what becomes of our boasting? It is excluded. By what kind of law? By a law of works? No, but by the law of faith. For we hold that one is justified by faith apart from works of the law. (Romans 3:27-28)*

Turning & Trusting

The required response to the gospel is a turning from sin to God and a transfer of trust from ourselves to Christ. In short, the call of repentance and faith is a call to turn and trust. God defines and illustrates these two components of the response to the gospel in the Bible, so that we will know what is required.

God's work in our hearts to get us to that point may take weeks, months or even years. But when it happens, it happens all at once – instantaneously. After months or even years of preparation, in a moment of time, God produces a changed orientation in our hearts. In one moment he draws us across the line, granting us the ability to ditch all of our confidence in our own resumé and enabling us to place our full trust in Christ.

This radical rearrangement of your trust and life's focus will be undeniable. It is a work of God in your spirit that cannot go unnoticed. Our biblical study in the last two chapters of what repentance and faith are and what they look like should make clear whether this has happened in your life or not. It is not a self-induced reshuffling of your ideas about God. It is a profound rearrangement of who you are. It is so profound that the Bible refers to it as a "new birth" (Jn.3:1-15). It is described as a new life, an entirely new kind of life, that God produces in us. It is a kind of "new birth" that the Bible says is *"not of the will of the flesh nor of the will of man, but of God"* (Jn.1:13).

This divinely induced turning and trusting is something Jesus describes in the following way:

> *"No one can come to me unless the Father who sent me draws him. And I will raise him up on the last day... It is the Spirit who gives life; the flesh is no help at all. The words that I have spoken to you are spirit and life. But there are some of you who do not believe."* (For Jesus knew from the beginning who those were who did not believe, and who it was who would betray him.) And he said, *"This is why I told you that no one can come to me unless it is granted him by the Father."* (John 6:44, 63-65)

If you truly have the desire to be right with God, to turn from sin and trust in the Jesus of the Bible, if you sense the draw to become a follower of Christ, realize that the triune God is thoroughly involved in the process. In the Bible Jesus is called *"the founder and perfecter of our faith"* (Heb.12:2). God the Father is described as the One who *"gives repentance to Israel and the forgiveness of sins"* (Ac.5:31) and *"to the Gentiles also God grants repentance that leads to life"* (Ac.11:18). We are told that, *"for the sake of Christ"* we have been *"granted to believe in him"* (Phil.1:29). The Holy Spirit is said to have been sent throughout the world to work on individuals and to *"convict them concerning sin and righteousness and judgment"* (Jn.16:8).

Those of us who have had this undeniable work in our lives recognize that God is to be credited and thanked, because when we turn from our sin to God and transfer our trust to Christ to receive forgiveness, we are doing something that only God can enable.

Critics may ask, "What about those who want to rightly respond to the gospel, but God doesn't enable them?" The answer is, that doesn't happen. Some may desire the benefits of being rightly related to God because they want the benefits associated with salvation, but they want Christ on their own terms - for example, the "rich young ruler" in Matthew 19 or the trio of would-be-followers in Luke 9:57-62. These individuals want to write their own terms for salvation and have Christ approve their terms and agendas. Clearly this is not the right response to the gospel. Real Christianity begins with a desire to "sign the blank check" and let Jesus fill in the terms. This is a desire that, if you have it, God has induced and he will always respond with granting a full pardon for your sins.

Prayers, Aisles, Signatures and Pinecones

At this point some will ask, "So what specifically do I do to become a Christian?" And unfortunately many well-meaning Christians inject a number of unbiblical answers: "You need to sign a commitment card," "You need to walk the aisle at the end of the church service," "You need to recite a sinner's prayer" or the old Christian camp directive, "You need to throw a pinecone in the fire to say 'God I'm yours.'"

The reality is, the work of repentance and faith is something that is generated by God internally. It is something that happens in your spirit. It is a moment of surrender to the work of God. It is a turning from sin to God and to trusting fully in Jesus Christ not yourself to save you from the penalty of your sin. By the time someone throws the pinecone, recites a prayer, or walks an aisle – if it is true repentance and faith – the "right response" has already taken place in his or her heart.

Not that an external expression of our internal repentance and faith is bad. It's just that "raised hands" and "signed cards" are not what God has prescribed. God has told all repentant, trusting new followers of Christ to be baptized in water as an expression of their new life in Christ.[6] This ancient practice, officiated by church leaders in Bible-teaching churches, is what God expects from those who have become "disciples of Christ." Here are Jesus' words as he prescribes

---

[6] See Larry E. Dyer's concise and helpful little book on water baptism, *Baptism: The Believer's First Obedience* (Kregel Publications, 2000). For a more thorough explanation of why water baptism is not what actually saves us and why only repentant and trusting followers of Christ, not babies are to be baptized see Thomas Schreiner and Shawn Wright's *Believer's Baptism: Sign of the New Covenant in Christ* (B & H Academic, 2007) and Matt Waymeyer's *A Biblical Critique of Infant Baptism* (Kress Christian Publications, 2008).

baptism as a perpetual practice for his people. *"Go therefore and make disciples of all nations, baptizing them in the name of the Father and of the Son and of the Holy Spirit"* (Mt.28:19). Notice carefully, we don't make disciples of Christ by baptizing them, we baptize "them" (i.e., "disciples) after they have already been made disciples by the proclamation of the gospel.

Of course God knew that water baptism would be a total initial indicator of the genuineness of one's faith. For someone to say, "I have rightly responded to the gospel and I am right with God, but I am too embarrassed to be baptized" instantly reveals the synthetic nature of his or her faith. For to say, "I trust Christ completely for my eternal salvation, but I cannot trust him to step out and be baptized next Sunday" is quite a contradiction. That's why Jesus so often looked to the expressions of our faith to prove the reality of our faith. Notice his forthright and diagnostic words in John 3, *"Whoever believes in the Son has eternal life; whoever does not obey the Son shall not see life, but the wrath of God remains on him"* (v.36). We cannot say that we genuinely "trust in him" if we are not willing to "obey him." And water baptism, not raised hands or recited prayers, is the first directed act of obedience. Peter, in the first sermon of the early church, even joined the required response to the gospel and baptism in the same sentence. After he preached the gospel the crowd cried out, *"What shall we do?"* to which Peter responded, *"Repent and be baptized"* (Ac.2:37-38).

So if, even while reading this book, God has worked in your heart genuine repentance and faith, find a good Bible-teaching church and talk to the pastor about scheduling your water baptism, so that you can express to other Christians that you have recently become a follower of Christ. Then it's time to start living for Christ in a way you never have before. It's time to follow Christ with the entirety of your life – every day of your life. Let's spend a little time understanding what that looks like and how the Bible would have us go about it.

Chapter 6
Good Works

I once owned a combination lock that I purchased to use at the gym. I knew the numbers were 29, 31 and 16. The problem was that because of the extended breaks between trips to the gym (as happens for some of us), I could rarely remember the correct order required to open the lock. Hopeful, I would enter 16... 31... 29. Then 16... 29... 31. Frustrated, I would try 31... 29... 16. As with any combination lock, it wouldn't work unless I had the right numbers *in the right order.* The elusive "31... 16... 29," came after several minutes of trial and error. Though I never forgot the numbers the sequence was critically important.

Christians strive to promote a biblical gospel, a right response to the gospel, and good works. Christians promote these things because the Bible presents them all as critically important. When it comes to the order of these three elements, there is no room for trial and error. Assuming the wrong sequence of these right things has a catastrophic result.

The Role of Good Works

We've considered the biblical gospel and the required response of repentance and faith. But now when we come to the important topic of good works, it is critical that we never take these three out of their proper sequence. As stated in the last chapter, good deeds in no way contribute to our salvation. We don't earn, merit or any way contribute to our reconciliation with God. It is God's gracious gift, which Christ has accomplished for us. Our good works are useless as a contributing factor to our forgiveness.

Yet, we dare not assume that they are not an essential part of the discussion concerning our right relationship with God. Notice the sequence and importance of our good works in the following passage.

> *For by grace you have been saved through faith. And this is not your own doing; it is the gift of God, not a result of works, so that no one may boast. For we are his workmanship, created in Christ Jesus for good works, which God prepared beforehand, that we should walk in them.*
> *(Ephesians 2:8–10)*

Our reconciliation with God is wholly accomplished by grace, it is an unearned gift. Our works do not contribute. And yet, the last sentence in the above paragraph makes an emphatic declaration that we are created by God's grace as reconciled followers of Christ for a specific purpose –good works. God has planned an entire set of them for us to accomplish.

The wrong arrangement:
The Gospel + Repentance/Faith + Good Works = Salvation

The biblical arrangement:
The Gospel + Repentance/Faith = Salvation + Good Works

God has saved you to live out an entire repertoire of biblical good works. He has done what was required to forgive you and to relationally associate you with him, so that your life would be lived in a way that brings him glory – puts the good of his agenda and values on display. You and the other Christians on the planet are said to be, *"a people for his own possession, that you may proclaim the excellences of him who called you out of darkness into his marvelous light"* so, the text goes on to say, *"abstain from the passions of the flesh"* and *"keep your conduct among the Gentiles honorable"* (1Pet.2:9-12). Considering all that God has done for us, we should be more than enthusiastic to do so. This is why Christ *"gave himself for us to redeem us from all lawlessness and to purify for himself a people for his own possession who are zealous for good works"* (Tit.2:14).

Our New Resources

As a reconciled person God has promised to be personally involved in your life. As Paul told the Christians at Philippi, *"work out your own salvation with fear and trembling, for it is God who works in you, both to will and to work for his good pleasure"* (Phil.2:12-13). God has so changed his relationship with you, that you now have a kind of connection with him which will empower and enable you to live a life you never thought possible.

All that I will talk about in this closing chapter, is made possible in our lives by what the Bible calls the indwelling of God's Spirit. Of course this is a spatial analogy. This means that God's Spirit will be so involved in my life, that he is described as not only being "with me" but "in me." God's indwelling Holy Spirit will spark a kind of conflict that will be hard to ignore. While we all struggle with the residual presence of old sinful impulses and ungodly appetites, the Spirit of God, because of his presence in us, is able to overpower these and create a new kind of lifestyle. Scripture says,

> *If the Spirit of him who raised Jesus from the dead dwells in you, he who raised Christ Jesus from the dead will also give life to your mortal bodies through his Spirit who dwells in you. (Romans 8:11)*

God's Spirit works in us to make us different people in the way we live, think, speak and behave, that's why Christians often call these new patterns the "fruit of the Spirit." As a Christian, though your old desires will still *"wage war against your soul"* (1Pet.2:11), God's Spirit in you will work to fight them back. The Bible describes the battle this way:

> *But I say, walk by the Spirit, and you will
> not gratify the desires of the flesh. For the
> desires of the flesh are against the Spirit, and
> the desires of the Spirit are against the flesh,
> for these are opposed to each other, to keep
> you from doing the things you want to do.
> But if you are led by the Spirit, you are not
> under the law. Now the works of the flesh
> are evident: sexual immorality, impurity,
> sensuality, idolatry, sorcery, enmity, strife,
> jealousy, fits of anger, rivalries, dissensions,
> divisions, envy, drunkenness, orgies, and
> things like these. I warn you, as I warned you
> before, that those who do such things will
> not inherit the kingdom of God. But the fruit
> of the Spirit is love, joy, peace, patience,
> kindness, goodness, faithfulness, gentleness,
> self-control; against such things there is
> no law. And those who belong to Christ Jesus
> have crucified the flesh with its passions and
> desires. (Galatians 5:16–24)*

As we "walk in step" with God's Spirit and cling to Christ in our hearts and minds, the presence of God in our lives will "bear fruit" that is in opposition to the old way we used to live. God makes this possible. I wish I could report that we do this with perfection, but unfortunately we don't. God is always at work, convicting us and provoking a new kind of guilt and dread when we fall – and we will fall. There are episodes of sin in the Christian life (sometimes bad ones), but if we are truly right with God, he will not allow those to continue. He will get involved in a strong and undeniable way, to bring our episode of sin to an end.

> If we say we have no sin, we deceive ourselves, and the truth is not in us. If we confess our sins, he is faithful and just to forgive us our sins and to cleanse us from all unrighteousness. If we say we have not sinned, we make him a liar, and his word is not in us. My little children, I am writing these things to you so that you may not sin. But if anyone does sin, we have an advocate with the Father, Jesus Christ the righteous. (1 John 1:8–2:1)

The good news is, as Christians, God actively works *in* our bouts with sin. Like a father, God the Father will swiftly deal with our stumbling.

> God is treating you as sons. For what son is there whom his father does not discipline? If you are left without discipline, in which all have participated, then you are illegitimate children and not sons. Besides this, we have had earthly fathers who disciplined

> us and we respected them. Shall we not much
> more be subject to the Father of spirits and
> live? For they disciplined us for a short time
> as it seemed best to them, but he disciplines
> us for our good, that we may share his
> holiness. For the moment all discipline seems
> painful rather than pleasant, but later it
> yields the peaceful fruit of righteousness to
> those who have been trained by it.
> (Hebrews 12:7–11)

This is why real Christians cannot continue in prolonged seasons of sin. God will always get involved. Non-Christians, even churchgoing people, can sin and continue to sin without God's intervention. But real children of God cannot. As the Bible says, *"no one who keeps on sinning has either seen him or known him... No one born of God makes a practice of sinning, for God's seed abides in him, and he cannot keep on sinning because he has been born of God"* (1 Jn.3:6, 9).

A New You

The difference is not only the presence of God in your life, though that alone is huge, the Bible says that there is also something else, which has significantly changed who you are. There is a fundamental conversion in your spirit that changes your core desires, your default direction in life and the way you think.

The words of 2 Corinthians 5:17 are profound: *"If anyone is in Christ he is a new creation, the old has passed away; behold the new has come."* The Old Testament describes how God looked forward to this radical transformation in the lives of his people with this dramatic description:

> *I will give you a new heart, and a new spirit I will put within you. And I will remove the heart of stone from your flesh and give you a heart of flesh. And I will put my Spirit within you, and cause you to walk in my statutes and be careful to obey my rules.* (Ezekiel 36:26–27)

Along with the indwelling Spirit of God (capital "S") there was the promise that when we are made right with God we will get a new spirit (small "s"), which is as different from our old one as rock is from flesh. Our internal life is transformed. Before our reconciliation we are "dead" to God, unresponsive to his will, but after it we are made right with him. Now his Spirit works alongside our new spirit so that we live life with a new kind of care and concern for doing what God wants.

As God promised through the pen of Jeremiah, *"I will put my law within them, and I will write it on their hearts"* (Jer.31:33). When God gives us a new spirit it is as though the God of the universe has written his directions, precepts, values and rules on our hearts.

Good Works

Now when we read the Bible, our hearts resonate with what it is directing us to do. Before our reconciliation, our hearts are described as being in rebellion to God's laws, but now our hearts are reprogrammed to beat in sync with his laws.

Because of the Holy Spirit and our new spirit, the New Testament can confidently state, *"Whoever keeps his commandments abides in God, and God in him. And by this we know that he abides in us, by the Spirit whom he has given us"* (1 Jn.3:24). This is a new capacity, a new enablement that comes from a reprogramed heart and from the resident Author of the Bible actively interacting with our heart and mind.

Again, it is important to point out that while the internal core of a Christian is a "new creation," every Christian currently lives in an "old shell," which the Bible frequently calls "the flesh." The flesh is more than our physical body. It is the whole of our fallen, currently unredeemed humanity. And since our remade spirit and our fallen human bodies are so intertwined, there is an internal conflict within every Christian that is quite profound. *"The spirit is willing"* to obey and serve God, that is precisely what it wants, but *"the flesh is weak"* and uncooperative –to put it mildly (Mt.26:41). The fleshly humanity in which all Christians live produces a kind of hostility that makes perfect Christian living impossible. While some followers of Christ will demonstrate an impressive trajectory as it relates to obedience, there will always be those episodic failures, which will disgust and repulse their new hearts.

We need to be prepared for this internal battle. It will be a ruthless conflict, wherein we must deny our sinful bodily appetites and desires. Scripture describes this battle with our sinful desires, as working to "put them to death."

> *So then, brothers, we are debtors, not to the flesh, to live according to the flesh. For if you live according to the flesh you will die, but if by the Spirit you put to death the deeds of the body, you will live. (Romans 8:12–13)*

This is all aptly summarized by Paul's exhortation to the Colossian Christians.

> *Put to death therefore what is earthly in you: sexual immorality, impurity, passion, evil desire, and covetousness, which is idolatry. On account of these the wrath of God is coming. In these you too once walked, when you were living in them. But now you must put them all away: anger, wrath, malice, slander, and obscene talk from your mouth. Do not lie to one another, seeing that you have put off the old self with its practices and have put on the new self, which is being renewed in knowledge after the image of its creator. (Colossians 3:5–10)*

The good news is that this internal fight with our fallen human desires will one day be over. For Christians, the final victory over these struggles soon becomes one of our most profound expectations. Though our inclusion in God's family is settled at our conversion, the completion of our "adoption" won't be until we receive redeemed, remade and recreated bodies. Romans 8:23 says, *"we ourselves, who have the firstfruits of the Spirit, groan inwardly as we wait eagerly for adoption as sons, the redemption of the body."* One day our "flesh" will no longer fight the desires of the Spirit. This is why Paul can enthusiastically write, *"to live is Christ, to die is gain"* (Phil.1:21). Of course the day of our graduation is up to God, so we must continue to live each day for Christ until he takes us home.

The Call to Obedience

It is not uncommon to find the gospel presented alongside an immediate call to obedience. That is because true repentance and faith always produce obedience. Real repentance brings a change in our lives. Paul reported on his evangelism by saying that he called people to *"repent and turn to God, performing deeds in keeping with their repentance"* (Ac.26:20). John the Baptist told his hearers, *"Bear fruit in keeping with repentance"* (Mt.3:8). It was said of the Thessalonian converts that everyone who saw their lives reported *"how [they] turned to God from idols to serve the living and true God"* (1Th.1:9).

Regarding faith the Bible says,

> *What good is it, my brothers, if someone*
> *says he has faith but does not have works?*
> *Can that faith save him? ···faith by itself, if it*
> *does not have works, is dead. But someone*
> *will say, "You have faith and I have works."*
> *Show me your faith apart from your works,*
> *and I will show you my faith by my works.*
> *(James 2:14–18)*

Real faith and real repentance are going to result in a life of increasing obedience to God. While some want to forego any discussion of good works during evangelism for fear that some may think good works contribute to salvation, the Bible doesn't share that strategy. Yes, it is imperative that we maintain the proper sequence in everyone's mind, but we should avoid the error of not presenting all the pertinent elements of the good news in our evangelism.

Therefore, another wrong arrangement of the elements is:

The Gospel + Repentance/Faith = Salvation

Because God wants everyone to know that becoming a Christian will necessarily initiate a life of good works, we must continue to preach a gospel that tells people:

The Gospel + Repentance/Faith = Salvation + Good Works

This is extremely helpful and clarifying for those who are under the false impression that they have been reconciled to God, but whose lives remain unchanged. The Bible is full of clarifications that you are lying to yourself if you think God has invaded your life and given you a new heart, but there is no evidence of this change. The Bible unabashedly says, *"Whoever says 'I know him' but does not keep his commandments is a liar, and the truth is not in him"* (1Jn.2:4) and "*If we say we have fellowship with him while we walk in darkness, we lie and do not practice the truth"* (1Jn.1:6). The last thing we want to do is give the false impression that getting right with God may or may not change one's life – it always does.

The gospel radically changes lives, even if the person had externally conformed to a set of Christian values prior to his conversion. Having one of these testimonies myself, as a compliant kid raised in church, I know the difference between external conformity and internal transformation. Saying "no" to sin can be done for a variety of reasons and some churchgoers can reform their own behavior, but these changes are always from the outside-in. Getting right with God changes us from the inside-out. It is a new kind of obedience that springs from a new heart.

It is doing the right things for the right reasons. It is a new pattern of internal obedience, which works its way out into every part of our lives. Those who have been "born again" can attest to the distinction between these kinds of good works.

A Lifetime of Change

Jesus spent a lot of time illustrating the kind of lasting "fruit" that endures. He spoke of temporary "fruit" that springs from artificial faith, as compared to the ongoing nature of "fruit that abides" (Jn.15:17). At other times he taught about differing soils, representing differing people who, in response to the gospel, produced "no fruit" or "temporary fruit." He contrasted these with a kind of soil that "bears fruit" for the long haul. Of course, the soil that bears fruit produces it in differing measures (some thirtyfold, some sixtyfold and some hundred fold), but all of the soil that produced fruit, continued to bear fruit (see Mt.13, Mk.4 and Lk.8).

One of the most dangerous misunderstandings in modern Christianity is thinking that those who bail out of Christianity, after an enthusiastic yet short-lived stint "in the faith," are genuine Christians. The Bible goes to great lengths to explain that "temporary Christians" are not genuine Christians. In speaking of the second kind of "soil" Jesus said,

"And these are the ones sown on rocky

> *ground: the ones who, when they hear the*
> *word, immediately receive it with joy. And* .
> *they have no root in themselves, but endure*
> *for a while; then, when tribulation or*
> *persecution arises on account of the word,*
> *immediately they fall away." (Mark 4:16–17)*

The Luke account tells us that Jesus called these "tribulations or persecutions on account of the word" a "time of testing" (Lk.8:13). Unfortunately, the testing for these individuals proved their faith to be artificial. Elsewhere we are told that these trials come for the distinct purpose of showing us whether we are genuine Christians or not.

> *...you have been grieved by various trials,*
> *so that the tested genuineness of your faith—*
> *more precious than gold that perishes though*
> *it is tested by fire—may be found to result in*
> *praise and glory and honor at the revelation*
> *of Jesus Christ. (1 Peter 1:6b–7)*

<u>Real faith endures because it is a kind of faith that reflects a genuine relationship with Christ.</u> And according to Jesus:

> *"My sheep hear my voice, and I know them,*
> *and they follow me. I give them eternal life,*
> *and they will never perish, and no one will*

> *snatch them out of my hand. My Father, who has given them to me, is greater than all, and no one is able to snatch them out of the Father's hand."* *(John 10:27–29)*

This is why longevity in the faith is the continually stated proof that one's salvation is real. And why Paul could write, *"Now I would remind you, brothers, of the gospel I preached to you, which you received, in which you stand, and by which you are being saved, if you hold fast to the word I preached to you"* (1Cor.15:1-2). "Holding fast" to Christ doesn't save you, but those who are saved continue to hold fast. Elsewhere we are told, *"For we have come to share in Christ, if indeed we hold our original confidence firm to the end"* (Heb.3:14). It doesn't tell us "we will" share in Christ, if we hold our original confidence firm to the end. It says "we have" come to share in Christ, if we hold our original confidence firm to the end. Holding on to the end doesn't save us. But those who are saved hold their confidence firm to the end.

I say this is a dangerous misunderstanding among Christians, because far too many think that their friends or family members who have cast off their confidence in Christ, turned their backs on Christ, or bailed out of Christianity are "okay" because at some past point in time they appeared to, as Jesus put it, "receive the word with joy." They may have had a positive initial reaction to the gospel, but it wasn't a divinely induced response, because genuine repentance and faith will always produce a lifetime of fruit-bearing.

Again, this obviously does not mean that Christians live perfectly every day for the rest of their lives. There are plenty of bad days and some arduous seasons of paltry fruit, but the Bible tells us that real Christians have God abiding in them and that he is at work in them "both to will and to work for his good pleasure" (Phil.2:13).

The point is that you should never be tempted to think your faith is real if you find it only lasts for a while. You should expect, that if God has worked genuine repentance and faith in your heart, he will continue to work in and through you to bear fruit and you will continue to make measurable progress in becoming more and more like Christ (2Cor.3:18; Rom.8:29-30).

Ready for a Fight

Not only is there the current struggle of fighting the desires of our fallen humanity, but becoming a reconciled follower of Christ will also initiate a whole new kind of enmity with our sinful culture and its spiritual head. The New Testament is filled with cautionary words regarding the very real opposition we will face from fallen spiritual forces. God's spiritual enemies become ours. And they are said to be actively looking for ways to trip us up.[1] The Bible warns,

> *be sober-minded; be watchful. Your*
> *adversary the devil prowls around like a*
> *roaring lion, seeking someone to devour.*
> *Resist him, firm in your faith, knowing that*
> *the same kinds of suffering are being*
> *experienced by your brotherhood throughout*
> *the world. (1 Peter 5:8–9)*

One of the most effective means used by the enemy to attack our faith, is the world's system in which we live. The world's cultures are certainly not designed to foster and encourage our relationship with Christ. And that is by design! The world's values, acclaim, media and entertainment are constructed to work against our spiritual growth. Undoubtedly we have to live in the world, but the Bible tells us that we need to be ready not to fit in like we used to. This reality couldn't be made any clearer than in these words from Christ,

"*If you were of the world, the world would*

---

[1] C.S. Lewis' creative depiction of these types of spiritual battles in *The Screwtape Letters* (Barbour Publishing, 1990) is worth the read. More systematic works on the topic include Fred Dickason's *Angels: Elect and Evil* (Moody Press, 1975) and Robert Lightner's *Angels, Satan & Demons* (Word Publishing, 1998). For an appropriate warning against an obsession with spiritual forces see Thomas Ice's *Overrun by Demons: The Church's New Preoccupation with the Demonic* (Harvest House, 1990).

> *love you as its own; but because you are not*
> *of the world, but I chose you out of the*
> *world, therefore the world hates you.*
> *Remember the word that I said to you:*
> *'A servant is not greater than his master.'*
> *If they persecuted me, they will also persecute*
> *you." (John 15:19–20a)*

Jesus often followed these sobering warnings with an optimistic encouragement that it is not only possible to survive, but we can actually thrive. God has given us what is needed to "overcome" this continual pushback. God himself indwells and empowers his church and *"the gates of hell will not prevail against it"* (Mt.16:18b). Yes, *"in the world you will have tribulation"* but Christ says, *"take heart; I have overcome the world"* (Jn.16:33).

We just need to be ready to have a very different relationship with the world than we had before. We can't fit in comfortably. We can't just relax and "go with the flow." We need to push against the pressure to be like everyone else. You need to consciously work to *"not be conformed to this world, but be transformed by the renewal of your mind"* (Rom.12:2). And that renewal comes through one primary source!

Getting in the Word

The Bible is God's unalterable, inscripturated revelation to us concerning himself, his gospel and how we Christians are to live to bring glory to him. As such, the Bible must become a daily part of our lives. We need to read it, study it and commit sections of it to memory. It will be God's tool to keep our mind renewed in a world that is seeking to conform us to its way of thinking.

Those who love God, love his written word. God produces this love for his word and will drive us back to it frequently. A read through the longest song in the Bible will overwhelm you with this perspective. Here is a sample from Psalm 119 of the love God's people have for his word.

> ...my heart stands in awe of your words. I rejoice at your word like one who finds great spoil. I hate and abhor falsehood, but I love your law. Seven times a day I praise you for your righteous rules. Great peace have those who love your law; nothing can make them stumble. I hope for your salvation, O Lord, and I do your commandments. My soul keeps your testimonies; I love them exceedingly. (Psalm 119:161b–167)

This love for God's word is one of the evidences of true spiritual life. It is part of the fruit which proves that we are genuinely converted people. So dig in daily and fill your spiritual appetite for God's word the way you would schedule and work to feed your daily hunger for food. There are many helpful books available written to provide you with workable methods of Bible study.[2] Choose a time, a place and a solid method for systematic study and get started.

Connections with God's People

God has organized and structured a place in which Christians can grow. Christ's church has been built by God and scattered throughout the world for the purpose of fostering and promoting a growing team of Christ followers. While no church is perfect, God calls you to find the best one you can find within a reasonable distance and get plugged in. We were not designed to live the Christian life alone. Impromptu meetings with others are not enough. God has constructed and arranged churches under the leadership of mature and qualified leaders to be the place where Christians learn and bear fruit as a team.

The Bible calls the church the *"household of God, which is the church of the living God, a pillar and buttress of the truth"* (1Tim.3:15). The church is where the truth is to be boldly proclaimed and upheld in a world filled with lies and deception. From the church, God's life is to be shone forth to penetrate a dark culture. That is why a good church is such an appropriate place to corporately bear fruit for God's

---

[2] See for instance, Howard and William Hendrick's *Living by the Book* (Moody Press, 2007); Gordon Fee and Douglas Stuart's *How to Read the Bible for All It's Worth* (Zondervan, 1982); and Andy Deane's *Learn to Study the Bible* (Xulon Press, 2009).

glory. It will be a place where you are encouraged and spurred on to live for him. Don't dismiss church and don't neglect it. As God's word says,

> *let us consider how to stir up one another to love and good works, not neglecting to meet together, as is the habit of some, but encouraging one another, and all the more as you see the Day drawing near.*
> *(Hebrews 10:24–25)*

Some are tempted to think that the more they mature in Christ, the less they need their church. This is not true. According to Hebrews 10:25, the opposite is the case. As the final Day draws near we are told to gather "all the more." Church will be the place where God will use your life to be a motivation and an encouragement in the lives of others. It is an organization that will utilize your growing knowledge of God's word to counsel and instruct your brothers and sisters in Christ. The church is an indispensible part of God's plan to produce good works in and through your life. So be sure you get involved and stay involved.

A Brief Epilogue for Christian Evangelists

I am personally concerned that the biblical gospel has been truncated, eviscerated and shrink-wrapped to fit nicely into the sound-byte arsenal of the evangelist on the go. The problem is that pairing down the good news is a hazardous endeavor. After hearing abbreviated deliveries of the gospel, people are left to themselves to fill in the blanks, redefine words and concepts, and to employ their own set of implications.

Yes, there are certain times when we find ourselves in one of those brief encounters where we have little option but to summarize what God has said about getting right with him. But even then, we need to make sure that we are speaking of the biblical gospel in biblical terms. It is critical that as good ambassadors we don't substitute words like "sin," "repentance" and "faith" with the all-too-common, cute and trite churchgoer phrases. "Asking Jesus into your heart" will never substitute for God's command to turn from sin and trust exclusively in Christ's finished work. And "Jesus loves you" won't come close to communicating the real problem of our sin and how God in Christ paid the incalculable price as our substitute on the cross.

I encourage you to keep a set of inexpensive Bibles

or pocket New Testaments handy that you can give to your evangelistic prospects to read, as a follow up to those divinely appointed conversations.[1] Ask them to read the gospel of Luke or the book of Romans and schedule another time to meet with them or call them to discuss what they have read. Nothing is more effective than getting non-Christians to actually read God's word for themselves. You may be intimidated about offering to field their questions, but offer to do so anyway. This will allow you to quickly discover whether they are simply looking to make excuses for ignoring God's call or if God is actually preparing their heart to respond to his message of reconciliation. If God is, their questions will likely be ones you can relate to and aptly answer. If a question does stump you, remember that you are not in a staged debate or a battle of egos. Tell them you need to look into it, do your homework, and get back to them.

It was my hope in writing this book, that when it comes to the component parts of the gospel the preceding pages might help to guide your evangelistic prospects to think through something of the breadth of our human problem and the great lengths to which God has gone to solve our real problem in Christ. It is my prayer that you might use *Getting It Right* as a supplement to your evangelism, giving it out to those you speak to, as a way of reinforcing what you have

---

[1] Many Bible publishers provide materials at no cost. Crossway will provide multiple copies of their ESV Bibles at no cost, if they are used for evangelistic purposes. Go to www.Crossway.org.